RINGNECK!

Pheasants
and Pheasant
Hunting

BOOKS BY TED JANES:

A Boy and His Gun
Freshwater Fishing Complete
A Boy and His Boat
First Book of Camping
When Cape Cod Men Saved Lives
When Men Dug Gold in the Klondike
Wilderness Warden
Trouble at Clear Lake
Salmon Fishing in the Northeast
Camping Encyclopedia
I Remember Cape Cod

RINGNECK!

*Pheasants
and Pheasant
Hunting*

by E. C. JANES

*CROWN PUBLISHERS, INC.
NEW YORK*

Printed in the United States of America
Published simultaneously in Canada by General Publishing Company Limited

Designed by Ruth Smerechniak

Library of Congress Cataloging in Publication Data

Janes, Edward C
    Ringneck! : Pheasants and pheasant hunting.

    1. Pheasant shooting. 2. Ring-necked pheasants. I. Title.
SK325.P5J36   1975   799.2'48'61   75-157- 48

ISBN 0-517-52321-3

To Lurton Blassingame,
author's representative, sportsman, and good companion afield

Contents

Foreword

When, after several experiments, Chinese ring-necked pheasants were successfully stocked in American covers, most gunners were enthusiastic. However, in various parts of the country, especially the East, there were some reservations, and even today there are those who profess to regard the pheasant as a sort of interloper or a johnny-come-lately trying to usurp the niche long occupied by the aristocrats of American game birds, the ruffed grouse and the woodcock. Since the pheasant does not thrive in the southland, there has never been the same conflict between it and the bobwhite quail.

To this hard core of reactionaries, the pheasant is a kind of second-class citizen, tolerated in its place but hardly to be considered seriously as a game bird. Curiously, however, I have never known one of these detractors to hold his fire when a cock pheasant clattered up in front of him in a grouse or woodcock cover—as they frequently do—or to fail to manifest satisfaction with his encounter unless, of course, he misses, as he frequently does.

Perhaps this patronizing attitude is not to be wondered at. Yankees have not always taken kindly to immigrants. Dutch, Germans, Swedes, Irish, Italians, Poles—all had to prove themselves before being accepted, and sometimes the acceptance was long deferred.

So, like the rest who came to these shores from foreign lands, the pheasant has had to prove itself and, as far as most of us are concerned, it has done so admirably. It has shown that it can adapt to civilization and climatic conditions over large sections of the country. It has demonstrated its ability to face changing times and changing ways, predation, hunger, disease, storms, and other adversities—and come up flourishing. Its challenging crow sounds in swales and swamps from which the grouse's drumming has long been absent. And over the years the pheasant has also shown itself to be a worthy adversary for the hunter and his dog, using legs as well as wings to circumvent its pursuers. As a result, it has become by all odds the number one game bird throughout its range.

This is not meant to detract one whit from the admitted status of ruffed grouse and woodcock as magnificent game birds. I yield to no man in my love of hunting them. These remarks are meant, rather, to give the equally worthy ring-necked pheasant its rightful place in the American hunting scene.

In more than a half century of upland gunning, I have witnessed many changes in my hunting circumstances. I have seen woods change to housing developments and fields to industrial parks, and have seen superhighways bisect former swales. In that time grouse and woodcock have been pushed farther and farther back into disappearing woodlands, but pheasants still remain in their accustomed haunts, even though today some of these haunts are off limits to hunters. In the open covers the shooting is as good today as it was a score or more years ago.

In writing this book about pheasants and pheasant hunting, I am indebted to many persons—to game management personnel of the Massachusetts Division of Fisheries and Game, the Oregon State Game Commission, the Nebraska Game and Parks Commission, the South Dakota Department of Game, Fish, and Parks, and the Pennsylvania Game Commission.

Also, to a number of cooperative individuals at Savage Arms Corporation, Remington Arms Company, Inc., Winchester-Western, and the Ithaca Gun Company.

I am likewise grateful to a score or more veteran pheasant hunters and their dogs across the land with whom I have spent pleasant days afield and from whose experience and knowledge I have profited greatly. And to my own good dogs, Dinty, Jake, Dart, Ruff, and Roby, who have taught me much concerning pheasant hunting.

And, finally, I am indebted to the pheasants themselves for leading me many miles through swamp and swale in their pursuit, sometimes successfully, sometimes unsuccessfully, but always with pleasure and enthusiasm. From them I have learned most of all.

E. C. Janes
Westfield, Massachusetts

RINGNECK!

*Pheasants
and Pheasant
Hunting*

The Gaudy Immigrant

Few game birds can claim a more ancient or more illustrious lineage than the ring-necked pheasant. According to legend, when Jason and the Argonauts brought the golden fleece back to Greece from Colchis, a country on the eastern shore of the Black Sea, they also brought with them some handsomely colored birds they had found on the banks of the Phasis River in Colchis. Hence the scientific name *Phasianus colchicus*—pheasants. So much is legend, but the fact that the native pheasants of the region today closely resemble the birds first introduced into Europe gives credence to this fabulous story of the pheasant's origins.

Apparently, pheasants flourished in Greece and some of their descendants were transported to Rome, where they were mentioned by the ancient writers Virgil, Catullus, and Pliny. Roman legions are thought to have introduced them into Britain at some later date.

There in A.D. 1059 King Harold described one "phasianus" as the alternative to two partridges among the rations at Waltham Abbey. Following this early reference to the birds in England we find several others over the years. In a book called *The Forme of Cury,* compiled in 1381 by the chief cook of King Richard, there is a recipe which describes how "fare to broile a fesant." And King Henry VIII included among his household retainers a French priest whose primary duties were those of "fesaunt breder." Apparently pheasant hunting, with crossbows, nets, and falcons, had already become a sport, and even in those early days, dogs must have played their part in the hunts. In 1677 an engraving by Holar has beneath it the lines:

> The Feasant Cocke the woods doth most frequent
> Where Spaniels spring and perche him by the scent.

It was this English pheasant that Governor Wentworth and Richard Bache, son-in-law of Benjamin Franklin, introduced on Wentworth's New Jersey estate in 1790. Earlier, George Washington, in between fighting the Revolution and becoming the nation's first president, had also liberated a few pheasants at Mount Vernon. But his efforts to establish them there failed, and so did the experiment of Wentworth and Bache.

It wasn't until almost a century later, in 1881, that the first successful pheasant-stocking program was carried out in America. In that year Judge Owen N. Denny, American consul general in Shanghai, obtained twenty-eight pheasants that were liberated on his estate in the shadow of Peterson's Butte in the Willamette Valley of Oregon. These birds were a nearly pure strain of Chinese pheasant (*Phasianus torquatus*). Other birds were introduced later; these stockings established themselves so well that eleven years later on the first day of the first open season fifty thousand pheasants were bagged.

Meanwhile, several other pheasant species had been introduced into England and, interbreeding with the original strain, produced a fertile hybrid. The principal bird involved in this mixture was the Japanese pheasant (*Phasianus versicolor*) brought to England via Europe by the earl of Derby in 1840. This hybrid, known still as the English pheasant, is a larger bird than the original and is also said to be more sporting to hunt and tastier to eat.

The first English pheasants liberated in America, following the unsuccessful earlier attempts, were introduced in New York State by Rutherford Stuyvesant in 1887 and finally became established after several tries.

In 1894 Samuel Forehand of Worcester, Massachusetts, obtained some pheasants from the Oregon flock. They were turned over to chairman Brackill of the Massachusetts Commission of Fisheries and Game, who used them as breeding stock, and later he released their progeny to populate Bay State covers. Twelve years later, in 1906, Massachusetts opened its first pheasant season during which several thousand birds were bagged.

By the turn of the century a number of states had initiated pheasant-stocking programs. In the course of their operations the Chinese strain, imported by Judge Denny, became crossed with the English pheasants introduced into the East, and to complicate matters further, another strain, the Mongolian or black-necked pheasant (*Phasianus colchicus mongolicus*) was added to the mix.

Today there are probably no pure strains of any of these breeds, certainly not among those raised by private and state game farms. But the birds we know today have taken on some of the best characteristics of their forebears, and gunners nationwide are happy with the results which have accrued from these imports—the hardy, crafty, adaptable, and tasty bird known universally to gunners as the ring-necked pheasant and to scientists as *Phasianus colchicus torquatus*. Literally millions are bagged each year throughout their range, and it is safe to say that, with the possible exception of the cottontail rabbit, pheasants are the most popular of all upland game.

Just for the record, mention should perhaps be made of some of the other breeds of pheasants which exist, but are for the most part of only academic interest to the gunner—the Lady Amherst pheasant, the golden pheasant, the Japanese green pheasant, and the melanistic or black pheasant. Of these only the latter two are of any real concern to hunters. The green pheasant has been experimentally stocked in a few areas, but there is no reason to believe that it will ever seriously challenge the ringneck as America's favorite game bird.

Practically everyone, hunter or not, even those who have trouble distinguishing between a sparrow and a catbird, recognizes the cock pheasant, with its broad white collar and crimson eye patch, the gray blue of its upper wing coverts and rump, the light buff of its black-spotted flanks, and its long, pointed, golden tail, barred with black.

It seems incredible that such gaudy plumage is also protective coloration, but it is, as every gunner can attest. Somehow, the buff and gold, the black spots and bars—even the reds—blend into a background of autumn foliage. Even in open fields, for that matter, the cock pheasant's ability to play the artful dodger is amazing.

One time I was walking through a field of young rye on my way to a nearby swampy cover when my Brittany spaniel froze on point some forty yards ahead. The grass was nowhere more than seven inches high and, since the Brit was young, I felt sure he was pointing a sparrow or a rabbit.

However, he was staunch and intense, so I approached with gun ready. As I did, the dog broke and trailed for several yards before pointing again. This time I strained my eyes, caught by a sudden movement of the grass. Then with great difficulty I made out a cock pheasant, belly to earth, gliding like a colorful snake through the short grass. If he had remained motionless, I never would have seen him and had it not been for the dog, I never would have known he was in the field at all.

Fewer persons, perhaps, can identify the hen pheasant, in her modest brown garb, slightly mottled on the back and lighter below, and with a somewhat shorter barred tail. Some confuse her with the ruffed grouse, but the lack of a ruff and her pointed tail serve to distinguish the two.

Cock birds average thirty-three to thirty-six inches from beak to tip of tail and weigh from two and one-half to three pounds. Hens average about twenty inches in length and from two to three pounds in weight.

Most people who frequent rural areas are familiar with the cock pheasant's raucous mating crow, a double squawk which has been likened to the grating swing of a rusty gate. Besides this well-known challenging note, pheasants have other calls for conversational and warning purposes. Cock birds cackle hysterically when flushed. Hens cluck anxiously or reassuringly to their chicks. Both hens and cocks make crooning sounds to express contentment. Cock birds also repeat a soft "putt-putt" as they walk from place to place and produce throaty grunts when angry.

Pheasants flourish in a moderately cool climate, provided that the necessary food and cover to sustain them are present. They have always frequented rural rather than wilderness areas, preferring places where agriculture has opened up the land to various food crops.

Here the birds find a beneficial diversity of various types of cover—hayfields, hedgerows, and pastures for nesting, and swamps, brushy woodlots, and swales for roosting cover—all close to the grain, fruits, insects, and berries that make up their favorite items of diet. Indeed, no bird, with the possible exception of the bobwhite quail, is better adapted to civilization than the pheasant.

They cannot survive the hard winters of northern New England and other cold areas where deep snows bury their food supplies. And, for some reason, neither have they done well in the Deep South. They have found their ideal habitat in the grain- and fruit-growing states of the Midwest and West.

MATING AND NESTING

The first signs of mating activity appear as early as February when cock birds begin to display a belligerent attitude toward one another. Cocks crow at times year-round, but the most frequent and persistent crowing takes place in March and April when the males establish their territories. Territories consist of areas twenty to seventy acres in extent to which hens are called for mating and which the cocks defend against all other males. The battles which ensue between rival cocks during the breeding season are seldom, if ever, fatal, but frequently the antagonists become well bloodied about the head and neck. Cock pheasants have been known to do battle with barnyard roosters upon occasion, and even to mate with domestic hens,

A July clutch in a typical nest. Earlier layings tend to be larger, as many as a dozen or more. Courtesy, South Dakota Department of Fish, Game and Parks

turkeys, and peahens. The offspring of a pheasant–hen mating is common enough to have earned a name, the pero.

Cock pheasants are polygamous. In pen experiments, a single cock has been found to be capable of breeding as many as fifty hens. Professional breeders usually allow each cock six to eight hens, but under some conditions they acquire much larger harems in the wild. And in fact, pheasants can be hunted to a 1:10 spring sex ratio without affecting the overall population.

Nesting season reaches its peak in late May and early June through most pheasant range. Nests are crudely constructed, shallow, saucerlike depressions in the ground, sometimes thinly lined with down and bordered with dead grass, leaves, and twigs. They are usually located in a natural hollow in a field, hedgerow, orchard, or brushy pasture, in thick vegetation. Sometimes, however, pheasants will nest in fairly open areas, for example, on the edge of a wood, where a nest is often built against a tree trunk. Alfalfa fields and brushy pastures are favored places. Roadside nests are not infrequent, and there are some records of nests being built in low trees, but this is very unusual.

In the early part of the season, hens frequently drop eggs on the ground at random. Sometimes they will start a nest, lay a couple of eggs in it, and then abandon the whole project. And not infrequently several hens will lay eggs in a single nest. These are known to biologists as "dump nests," and often contain from twenty to thirty eggs. As the season progresses, however, the hens cease this random egg-laying and settle down to the serious business of nesting and rearing a family.

Clutches average from eight to sixteen eggs, smaller than domestic chicken eggs, and varying in color from a pale green blue to olive brown. This variation in color is due to the interbreeding of the various species. Chinese pheasants, for example, are said to lay bluish green eggs speckled with a deeper tint. Hens cover the eggs with their brood patch, a section of skin from which feathers were shed before the first egg was laid.

Incubation requires from twenty-three to twenty-five days, during which time the hens remain on the nests day and night except to feed and exercise. Occasionally, cock pheasants have been discovered taking their turn at incubating the eggs, but it is not a common practice. Egg fertility is usually high, with an average hatch of 90 percent. Even though the eggs may have been laid over a period of a week or more, the entire clutch will hatch almost simultaneously, usually within twenty-four hours. The sex ratio averages half males and half females.

Unless the first clutch of eggs is destroyed, which frequently happens, there is only one laying. However, if the first nest is broken up, the hen will lay another clutch of eggs, which accounts for the small chicks often seen late in the summer.

THE FIRST YEAR

At birth, pheasant chicks are covered with down, reddish buff to dark brownish yellow in color, with dark stripes along the back and a dark spot around the ears. They can troop along behind their mother almost as soon as they are hatched, and begin to feed on seeds and insects, like adults, almost immediately. As they move about from nest to water to feeding and roosting grounds, the mother clucks softly to keep them together—or when danger threatens, to send them scurrying into hiding beneath leaves and grass tangles. As with fawns, pheasant chicks are said to have no odor at this age, which might betray their presence to predators. And, like the grouse and certain other birds, the hen pheasant will often feign a broken wing, flopping and fluttering as she leads potential enemies away from her concealed brood.

Despite this maternal concern, there is almost invariably a loss of chicks in every brood. As many as 80 percent fall victim to the attrition of cold, rainy weather, predation, and disease during the first few weeks of life. After seven weeks, the average brood is reduced to about a half dozen birds. If undisturbed, these chicks will stay with their mother for two months or more.

As time goes on, the downy chicks fade gradually to yellowish white, showing buff on the breast and flanks. Some display a dark spot on the thighs. At about eleven weeks, a postnatal molt takes place and adult feathering begins. The molt is complete, except for the two pointed outer primary feathers. Actually, chicks undergo a virtually continuous molt during their first summer. Adult plumage begins to replace juvenile at about four weeks of age, and young cocks begin to show some color on neck and breast at two months. The molt continues until the chicks are about five months old.

By twenty weeks the young birds have become fully feathered in adult plumage. Their first winter plumage, except for the outer primaries, is so similar to that of the adult that the young and adults cannot be distinguished from one another by sight.

The young chicks begin to make short, weak flights in a few weeks, and at three months are able to fly with fair ability. During the late summer and early fall, broods gradually disperse, and the young birds are on their own.

Even as adults, they face a disadvantage in flying: pheasants have a low ratio of wing area to body weight, and to make up for it they have to flap their wings three times a second—faster than some ducks. Pheasants have been known to fly over two miles, but the average flight is only a few hundred yards, characterized by a steep takeoff to about twenty-five yards, after which they plane downward alternately gliding and beating their wings.

Adult Hen

1 Day *2 Weeks* *4 Weeks* *6 Weeks*

At birth, the pheasant chick is a three-by-three-inch ball of fluff with three dark stripes down its back, weighing about an ounce. Two weeks later its wings are almost entirely feathered, enabling the chick to make short, hopping flights. The head and breast are still mainly covered with down, but feathers are developing down the flanks and on its back. It now shows a one-inch tail. Its weight has more than doubled and it stands five and a half inches high.

At four weeks the bird appears to be fully feathered, except for some fuzzy down on its head. It flies well, and the innermost primary wing feather has already moulted. The chick is already a quarter the size of the hen and weighs six ounces.

Six weeks after hatching, the bird is fully feathered, and the males are beginning to show

8 Weeks *10 Weeks*

a rufus color around their neck and breast. Other male feather patterns are becoming apparent in the inner wing feathers and the males are beginning to outweigh the females (12 oz.–9¼ oz.).

At eight weeks, the male chicks are half the size of the hen, eleven inches high and twelve inches long, slightly larger than the females. Their red face wattles are beginning to show, and the rufus color of the breast is more prominent. At ten weeks, blotches of green appear on the males' heads, and blue green rump feathers are evident. The males outweigh the females substantially (24 oz.–16 oz.), and both of them are moulting the last of their flight feathers. They will continue to grow, and complete their adult plumage by the time they are eighteen weeks old, though they will not be sexually mature until the following year.

On his own: this young cock already shows signs of his full adult plumage, which will be complete in about two months. Courtesy, South Dakota Department of Fish, Game and Parks

They often will land on a dead run, eating up territory with strong eighteen-inch strides, head and tail held high. Pheasants are built for running; their long legs are reinforced by splintery sesamoid bones, which improve the pulling power of the ligaments and thigh muscles.

These birds have been endowed with remarkably acute hearing. The claim has been made, with documentation to support it, that during World War II, pheasants reacted to artillery fire so far away that the explosions were inaudible to the human ear. Wildlife management personnel sometimes explode firecrackers along a spring census route to obtain an estimate of the number of cocks in the area, since these birds usually respond to a loud noise by crowing. Many pheasant hunters have had the experience of hearing a cock crow following the sound of gunfire in the vicinity.

Pheasants' eyesight is also extremely keen. Quite as spooky as wild turkeys and almost as wary, they seldom let an enemy approach closely while there is cover into which to run, unlike the bobwhite and woodcock, which usually prefer to sit tight and depend upon their protective coloration for protection.

As winter comes on, pheasants tend to flock together in bands that are generally sexually segregated, although now and again cocks and hens may be found together. Several considerations determine the size of these bands, but the density of the pheasant population is by far the most important factor.

Since there are usually more hens than cocks left after the hunting season, hen flocks are apt to be larger. Sometimes as many as fifty or more birds may band together, although the average is nearer a half dozen to a dozen; cock birds more often gather in smaller groups of two or three. These winter flocks feed together during the day and roost together at night.

ROOSTING

In summer and fall, pheasants roost on the ground, but in cold weather they often resort to trees. On windy, stormy nights they are apt to roost in the lower branches and in good weather on the higher limbs. Young evergreens are often chosen. Pheasants may also light in low trees or on fence posts to dry off after a storm. Also, on winter days they may sometimes be seen budding in trees, like grouse, although it is not at all common.

Not all pheasants roost in trees during the winter. Many still frequent the brushy covers, swamps, and woodlots which they use in summer, and it is said that following ice and sleet storms, pheasants have occasionally been found with their tails frozen to the ground.

The daily comings and goings of pheasants, as well as their seasonal movements, are fairly circumscribed, determined chiefly by the accessibility of the various types of cover that fulfill their everyday needs. Shortly after dawn they leave their roosting covers to feed. The middle of the day they spend sunning, dusting, and resting before feeding again from late afternoon until dusk when they return to the roosting grounds. This daily routine may be altered by weather conditions, disturbance by predators, and the abundance or scarcity of food. On stormy days, for example, pheasants may feed intermittently throughout the daylight hours.

Pheasants are practically omnivorous, which is one of the reasons they can survive in fairly cold climates. Their diet varies widely in different areas and at different times of the year and is determined largely by availability.

Grain, fruit, berries, seeds, and insects comprise the main elements of their diet, supplemented by leaves, buds, moss, and other items in times of scarcity. Early spring is the lean season; winter supplies have been pretty well exhausted and fresh growth has not yet begun to appear.

Slowly, new vegetation emerges and insects hatch to provide food for the

The brood breaks up in late summer; after only two months these poults are fully fledged and able to take care of themselves, pheasant style. Courtesy, South Dakota Department of Fish, Game and Parks

winter-worn adults and the newly fledged chicks. Insects, greens, and weed seeds proliferate in summer, culminating in the plenty of autumn when grain, insects, fruit, and berries are to be found in profusion. With the onset of winter, hard times return and only the leftovers of the fall bounty remain —weed seeds rising on sere stalks above the snow, frozen apples, buds, moss, and grasses in spring sumps.

In former years there was considerable agitation among sportsmen's groups, as well as by individuals, in favor of feeding pheasants during the winter, and that clamor is not yet entirely stilled. However, it is now generally agreed by both wildlife management authorities and informed laymen that such feeding is unnecessary and unwise.

For one thing, the cost of supplying sufficient feed would be prohibitive. But even if it were not, no particular benefits would accrue from a feeding program. Pheasants have long since learned to adapt to living conditions without a handout from man. They do very well in all but the most extraordinary weather. As long as they can find some form of food to fill their crops, they will remain alive and well.

Even if there is no food available, research has shown that it takes almost a month for a pheasant to starve to death. Further studies have revealed that as long as some form of greenery—leaves, moss, buds, or grasses—is available, pheasants can live on it for three months, and remain in good condition. Finally, winter feeding tends to concentrate birds near the feeding areas, thus increasing their vulnerability to predators and disease.

In a study carried on in Massachusetts, it was found that the average pheasant's diet consisted of the following: 32.5 percent weed seeds, 26.3 percent grain, 19.6 percent insects, 10.0 percent fruit. Most of the grain was waste material, gleaned from harvested fields, much of the weed seed came from noxious plants, and large numbers of the insects were harmful. Cutworms were found to be a favorite morsel. In some of the midwestern states, of course, grain would have represented a proportionately larger ratio in the diet.

Insects found in pheasant crops included coddling moths, apple maggots, tent caterpillars, tussock moths, cherry lice, plant lice, June bugs, tree borers, house and blowflies, gypsy moths, brown-tail moths, and rose bugs, as well as caterpillars, worms, and slugs. At times pheasants also eat acorns, beechnuts, roots, alfalfa, sphagnum moss, and clover.

However, since they relish corn, apples, tomatoes, peaches, grapes, and various cultivated berries, they do indubitably cause some damage to farm crops, more in certain parts of the country than in others. The chief reports of crop damage come from the Midwest and West where pheasants are more numerous than in the East. And it is interesting to note that pheasants are more abundant in states that provide the largest grain and fruit crops.

A census of farmers in Michigan showed that 92 percent of those polled declared that crop damage caused by pheasants was slight. Most scientific studies have shown that pheasants do more good than harm and are, on the whole, beneficial birds.

A scant five months after hatching, he looks like this: a symphony of color; wary and determined to survive. Courtesy, Massachusetts Division of Fisheries and Game

PHEASANT MANAGEMENT

More than most birds, except for the bobwhite quail, the pheasant lends itself to management, both habitat management and artificial propagation and rearing. This is in large measure the secret of their successful introduction into new lands and their ability to thrive in them. There is little that can be done to build up grouse populations aside from improving feed and cover potentials—but pheasants are another matter.

Literally millions of pheasants are raised annually on state and private game farms, and by sportsmen's organizations and individuals. All of them, except for breeding stock, are liberated each fall on preserves, state public shooting grounds, and on open lands to provide targets for the army of upland gunners who hold them their favorite game bird, both in the covers and on the table. And one thing that makes these liberated birds so satisfying a quarry is the fact that, though hatched and reared in captivity, once released into natural covers they become, as far as hunting is concerned, practically wild birds. Newly liberated pheasants will hide, run, and flush with much of the craftiness and wariness of wild birds of the same age.

Tales are told of recently stocked pheasants hanging around the release site, appearing in farmyards, and approaching humans so near they might be hit over the head with a stick. However, these myths are hardly borne out by the facts as known to wildlife management personnel and gunners.

A friend of mine once purchased three cock pheasants from a game farm for the purpose of training his young setter. He intended to liberate them for the training session but felt sure that he would be able to find them again on other days. I suggested that quail might better serve his purpose, but he shook his head.

"I'll put 'em in good cover," he said, "and they'll stay there till the season opens."

For the release he chose a cover several hundred yards wide, bordered by a pine bluff, and a half mile or so long. I went along to watch the proceedings. At the last minute I mentioned the idea of rocking the birds and planting them in strategic spots, but again my friend demurred.

"I'll just let 'em go," he said. "They're as tame as chickens. They'll just flutter off into the swale and the dog will have a chance to find them under natural conditions. You hold Sam."

I held Sam while my friend opened the crate. One second the pheasants were there, the next, with indignant cackles, they had taken wing and sailed fast and far. Two disappeared over the pine knoll, and the third was still going strong when he reached the far end of the swale. Sam never found one of them.

Pheasants stocked on any given morning will instinctively take advantage of every scrap of cover available in moving from feeding grounds to resting areas. They will lead dog and gunner a chase and by nightfall will roost deep in swamps or brushy swales, almost exactly like their wild kin. It is true, however, that such birds are more vulnerable to disease and predators at first.

On game farms, pheasants are known to have lived eight years or more, but in the wild their life-span is much shorter. Studies show that about half of the total number of birds shot in any given year are killed soon after opening day of the hunting season. During the remainder of the season, however, the kill figures drop sharply. Perhaps 5 percent of cocks born in any spring survive for two or more years to become the crafty, evasive roosters that crow their derisive challenges from the heart of deep swamps and briar-choked upland woodlots.

2

The Killers

The subject of pheasant predators and predation should be approached with caution and open-mindedness. Yet in fact, few subjects have created more conflicts over the years, the battle lines, as usual, being sharply drawn along lines of self-interest.

On one side are the large numbers of hunters and farmers calling for the complete extermination of crows, hawks, owls, foxes, and other species which they regard as the implacable enemies of their sport or livelihood. On the other side is the army of nature lovers and bird watchers who would greatly prefer the annihilation of all hunters to any diminution in the ranks of what they conceive to be their furred and feathered friends.

Certain fallacies are manifest on both sides of the question. Is the hungry fox that steals upon a roosting pheasant and eats it on the spot really any more predatory than the hunter who shoots a pheasant and takes it home for dinner—even though the hunter has paid a license fee for the privilege of killing his bird? On the other hand, as everyone agrees, pheasants feed on farm crops such as corn, potatoes, berries, and fruits, and hence are themselves predators of sorts.

Can it be that man divides predators and nonpredators along gastronomic lines, arbitrarily decreeing any creatures he finds inedible to be predators and those more appetizing to be game species? Or is this oversimplification?

The truth of the matter, of course, lies somewhere between the short-sighted and sometimes fanatical views of the antagonists. More and more today, this middle-of-the-road course is the one being followed by thoughtful sportsmen, farmers, scientists, and nature lovers.

For one thing, we have come to realize that even were it beneficial to do so, it would be entirely impossible to wipe out the so-called predatory species. Lord knows we have tried, with bounty systems, traps, poison, and dynamite. But no predator has ever been exterminated by these means. They have been around a long time and have learned to adapt to man, no matter how hostile his attitude.

We are also learning that it would be extremely unwise to attempt to destroy any species, so interdependent are all of them, including man, upon one another. Loss of habitat has made far greater inroads upon wildlife populations, including predators, than have guns, traps, and bounties. As a result, not only game birds and animals, but also predatory species—wolves, foxes, owls, hawks, and the rest—are becoming scarcer. Now steps are being taken to conserve our diminishing supply of these species along with the others.

Instead of bounties, many states now have closed seasons on foxes, crows, wildcats, coyotes, hawks, owls, and other predators. This protection, of course, results in the loss of some game birds and animals, but it also helps to preserve to some extent, the balance of nature, that delicate equilibrium that has been so often shattered by man.

It is true that foxes, cats, and birds of prey perform a service by culling out weak, diseased, and crippled birds. It is true that much of the predators' diet consists of insects, rodents, and other less desirable species. It is also true, however, that they frequently kill healthy birds and mammals—even as man does.

It is my purpose in this chapter neither to attack nor defend predators, given all the ramifications of this complicated subject. It is the intention here to take a realistic viewpoint, to describe the predators most dangerous to pheasants, and to discuss objectively their impact upon pheasant populations.

Since pheasants are birds of the farmlands rather than the deep woods, it is the predators found close to civilization that cause the most destruction among ringnecks.

CROWS

Many pheasants fall victim to predation even before their life outside the egg begins. One destroyer of embryonic chicks is the ubiquitous crow. From his perch near the top of a tall tree his keen eyes scan the landscape, alert for any sight or sound that may spell food—a road-killed squirrel, a farmer planting grain, or the first thrust of sprouting plants across a greening field.

He catches a glimpse of motion as a hen pheasant leaves her nest to feed, far below at the edge of a brushy woodlot. Silently, on black wings he glides downward to land in the vicinity of the nest. It takes only seconds to find it, lodged in a hollow between the roots of a hemlock tree. With his sharp, strong bill he shatters the eggs and swallows their contents one after another —perhaps the entire clutch, perhaps only three or four if he is driven off by the returning hen.

The nesting season coincides with the time of year when food in the form of insects, grain, and other crops is still scarce, and at this time the eggs of ground- and tree-nesting birds undoubtedly comprise an important portion of the crow's diet.

Two other facts, however, must be taken into consideration: One is that both crows and wild pheasants are scarcer today than they were not too many years ago. The vast crow roosts of the past have been broken up and destroyed by dynamite, and the ranks of crows have been decimated by guns, traps, and poison. As a result, there are just not that many crows around today; in fact, crow shooters across the country are complaining of a scarcity of targets, in comparison with former years.

Also, pheasant nests provide only a small share of the egg diet of crows. Pheasant and grouse nests are somewhat harder to locate than those of many songbird and waterfowl species, and these without doubt offer wider opportunities for plunder. Therefore, it would seem that in most areas crows present no truly critical threat to pheasant populations.

FOXES

To determine the actual extent to which fox predations influence pheasant populations, an intensive study was initiated in 1963 by the state of South Dakota, one of the top pheasant-producing states in the country.

The study was planned by the South Dakota Cooperative Wildlife Research Unit at the request of the Department of Game, Fish, and Parks. It was designed to reveal the results of a fox control program in northern Clark County carried out jointly by the Department of Game, Fish, and Parks and the Bureau of Sport Fisheries and Wildlife. In 1964 the program was changed to provide for an expanded study under Pittman-Robertson Federal Aid Project W-75-R, research study F-8-2, to be undertaken in four separate areas of eastern South Dakota, prime pheasant range.

Intensive fox control began in January 1965 and ended in December 1969. In 1966 a second portion of the study was added to determine the predatory effects of raccoons, badgers, and skunks, as well as foxes, upon pheasant populations.

The original program began with two study areas in each of the four units, one where foxes were intensively controlled, the other a check area where no control was established. A third study area where the same three predators were controlled was added to each unit in 1966. Each study area covered one hundred square miles. Researchers were also interested in learning what effect predator control would have on the increase of rabbits and small rodents such as mice, shrews, and ground squirrels.

Strychnine, gas, gunning, and trapping were the methods used in controlling predators. Fox stomachs and uteri were also collected to gain information on diet choices and litter sizes.

The first part of the study, in which only foxes were controlled, showed no important effects upon pheasant, rabbit, and small rodent populations, even though some 83 percent of each year's fox population was destroyed. Jackrabbit populations, however, gained about 136 percent throughout the five-year period in the fox control area. In all, the statistics showed 19 percent more pheasants, 18 percent more cottontails, and 15 percent more small mammals.

However, the second portion of the study, in which skunks, raccoons, and badgers were controlled along with foxes, showed far different results. The average population differences on the controlled areas versus the uncontrolled check areas showed 132 percent more pheasants per year, 63 percent more jackrabbits, 50 percent more cottontails, and only 18 percent more small rodents. This would seem to exonerate the fox as the worst offender against pheasants. But he must still be accounted a predator.

Behind my former home in Lexington, Massachusetts, there were wide fields, some planted to corn and tomatoes, others grown to weeds and bordered by brushy woodlots. This ideal habitat was well populated by both wild and pen-reared pheasants that provided good hunting throughout the season.

One spring in my cross-country wanderings I came upon a newly dug fox den located on a sunny slope at the edge of a wood. The time was mid-May, but already the sandy entrance to the den was littered with scraps of fur, feathers, and bones, including those of pheasants.

I left the den untouched because I knew that if I were to molest it the parents would only move to another one, and also this one would afford unusual opportunities for observing fox family life throughout the summer, thereby gaining me some idea of the extent of their predations. I didn't approach the den again, fearful that its discovery might cause its owners to move. I did my watching through binoculars from a distance, and it was a most rewarding experience.

There were days when my vigils were in vain and the den remained seemingly deserted, but there were also days of success. There were times when I watched the six cubs leaping at one another, mauling and chewing in mock combat while their mother watched from a flat rock above the den. And there was an early morning when the dog fox came trotting through the birches with a crippled rabbit wriggling weakly in his jaws.

He carried it as gently as a bird dog retrieving a woodcock and set it down a short distance from the excited cubs. Then he lay down to observe as the youngsters pounced upon the feebly hopping cottontail and tore it to pieces. Soon they would be stalking and killing prey on their own.

And there was an afternoon when a shifting breeze betrayed my presence and a sudden low growl from the mother sent the cubs flying into the den as if the earth had swallowed them. Not until they were all safely inside did the vixen scramble into the burrow's mouth.

I never saw the dog fox bring home a pheasant, but an increasing litter of pheasant feathers around the entrance to the den as the summer went on proved conclusively that he had done so with some regularity. And since this was before the pheasant-stocking season, these must have been wild or carry-over game-farm birds. Some, I suppose, may have been sick, but none was crippled by hunters and it seems likely that most of the birds were healthy and uninjured.

I didn't have a chance to continue my observations through the gunning season, for by then the family had separated and the den was deserted. However, I am sure that a number of newly stocked and wounded birds fell prey that fall to both the parents and the cubs that by now were hunting on their own.

It would, of course, be difficult to say how many pheasants were killed by the parent foxes during the rearing season, but I am sure that a dozen would be a conservative figure. If you multiply this number by the estimated number of dens in a township, a county, or a state, it adds up to a considerable number of pheasants destroyed, especially if you take into consideration the fact that many of the victims are hens whose deaths result in the loss of a dozen or so chicks apiece.

Anyone who enjoys walking in the woods after a fresh snow has probably read the mute testimony of the fox's expertise as a killer of winter-bound birds. The dainty set of tracks one behind the other, zigzagging across a field, the crouch at the edge of a tangled thicket, the belly crawl, the sudden spring, the drops of blood and fluff of feathers on the matted snow are familiar sights on the winter trails.

RACCOONS

Raccoons, plentiful everywhere throughout their range, are efficient

predators of pheasant eggs and pheasants when they are available. Furthermore, this easy-going, droll-appearing character in his black highwayman's
mask, ambling along watercourses in his nocturnal search for fish, frogs,
crayfish, and insects, can be a vicious and bloodthirsty killer upon occasion.
I know a preserve owner who lost four hundred adult pheasants in one night
to a pair of raccoons that burrowed underneath a fence and slaughtered the
birds, apparently for the sheer joy of killing.

No such opportunities present themselves in the wild, but their tree-
climbing abilities and their nocturnal habits enable raccoons to snatch a
roosting ringneck now and again, even those that seek the shelter of trees.

HAWKS AND OWLS

Turning again to winged predators, we come to some of the most destructive agents of all—the hawks and owls. Among the former there are good
hawks and bad hawks. Shooting a hawk just because it is a hawk is both
thoughtless and unjust as well as being in many cases illegal.

Among the good guys of the hawk tribe is the broad-winged hawk, about
fourteen inches long with a wingspread from thirty-three to thirty-six
inches. The sexes are similar in coloration, and broad-wings can be distinguished from other hawks by the fact that the white bands of the tail are
the same width as the black bands.

These hawks range widely over a large part of the country from New
Brunswick and Saskatchewan to central Texas and the Gulf Coast, wintering chiefly from Florida to the tropics. A bird of deep, forested areas, the
broad-wing may often be seen perched motionless on some high branch or
stub, waiting patiently hour after hour for some movement below that may
betray the presence of prey. His diet consists largely of insects, mice, chip-
munks, red squirrels, snakes, frogs, and an occasional songbird.

Another "good" hawk is the marsh hawk, a fairly large bird twenty
inches long with a wingspread up to fifty inches or more. Its wings are
broad and rounded, its distinguishing feature is the white patch on its rump.
Found throughout North America, this is the hawk one often sees gliding
on set wings low over fields and marshes, sweeping back and forth in its
search for field mice, rabbits, lizards, snakes, and frogs.

Somehow, the red-shouldered hawk has gained the common name
"chicken hawk." This is a most unfortunate misnomer, for it is one of the
most beneficial members of the hawk family. It destroys countless rodents
and noxious insects and only very occasionally preys upon domestic fowl
or game birds.

A retiring denizen of deep woods and swamplands over the eastern half of the country from Canada to the Gulf of Mexico, this good-sized hawk can be identified by the light-colored patch toward the tip of the wing at the base of the primaries. The reddish shoulder patches that give it its name are not usually visible as a distinguishing field mark.

The red-shouldered hawk's relative, the red-tailed hawk, also carries the unfortunate and undeserved appellation "hen hawk." Occasionally, this big, broad-winged hawk does prey upon poultry, but only when other food is not available. It much prefers to wait silently on a limb until some squirrel, snake, mouse, mole, shrew, or rat comes along—then it pounces quickly on silent wings. Snakes are a favorite item of diet, and when other food is not available the red-tailed hawk will eat carrion. The reddish underside of its tail is the distinguishing feature of this hawk, which ranges from Saskatchewan and Newfoundland south to the Gulf of Mexico.

The rough-legged hawk is a far-northern dweller that only visits the United States in winter. It is broad winged like the other members of this family (the Buteos), but is larger and has longer wings than most. It can be distinguished by a white tail tipped by a broad black band. Its name derives from the fact that its legs are completely feathered to its toes.

Its flight is silent as an owl's and, like those birds, it prefers to hunt in the dusk and on moonlit nights, sweeping over snowy fields in quest of the field mice that provide the greater part of its diet. Rough-legged hawks never prey upon poultry or game birds.

The sparrow hawk, smallest and most brightly colored of all the hawks, is a member of the falcon family. Unlike most of its falcon relatives, however, this bird is beneficial to man.

Scarcely larger than a robin, it can be identified by its size and its rufous red tail, and also by its habit of hovering on rapidly beating wings over one spot. The sexes can be distinguished by the male's blue gray wings, as opposed to the female's chestnut wings barred with black. They have similar black-and-white face markings.

You will often see a sparrow hawk perched on a telephone pole, scanning the area below for a glimpse of some morsel of food. In summer its fare consists largely of insects, but in late fall and winter it turns to a diet of mice. During the spring nesting season it occasionally captures songbirds and, despite its miniature size, has been known to attack small chickens. But for the most part it contents itself with insects and mice. It is widely distributed from the Yukon and Hudson's Bay to the Gulf of Mexico east of the Rocky Mountains.

Swainson's hawk is a western bird, ranging from the far north to Argentina. In size and coloring it somewhat resembles the red-tailed hawk, although its wings are more pointed. It is a somewhat confusing hawk to identify since individuals appear in both light and dark phases and are often mistaken for red-tailed or rough-legged hawks. However, the dusky-colored undersides of the wings are a good identifying feature.

Swainson's hawk is often seen wheeling in slow circles over the plains in search of its favorite food, the spotted gopher, or various mice. Insects of several kinds round out its diet. It is said that small birds frequently nest in the same tree with these hawks, showing their complete lack of fear of this species.

All of these hawks are more beneficial than harmful. Most are protected by law in many states, and shooting them serves no useful end in the interests of conservation.

The remaining members of the family common to North America are less deserving of the gunner's forbearance, for they definitely constitute a major threat to small game animals and to birds. Pheasants are especially vulnerable to their depredations.

COOPER'S HAWK

Well toward the forefront of the "baddies" of the hawk tribe is the Cooper's hawk, owing to its abundance and wide distribution. It, too, is known as chicken hawk, and in this case the name is justly deserved, for it is one of the most destructive to domestic poultry and upland game birds of all hawks.

The Cooper's hawk averages about twenty inches in length with a wing-spread of twenty-nine to thirty-six inches. It is sometimes mistaken for the sharp-shinned hawk, but its rounded tail serves to distinguish it from the square-tailed sharpshin.

The Cooper's hawk is more a bird of the woods than are some of the other *Accipiters*, but it frequently leaves its customary haunts to make swift-winged forays against chicken yards or fields that pheasants are known to inhabit. Bold to the point of rashness, it will sometimes carry out its barnyard raids even when the farmer is nearby.

One later summer afternoon as my wife and I drove along a back road bordered by weed-grown fields, a Cooper's hawk rose from a tangled thicket beside the road carrying a half-grown pheasant in its talons. Apparently our approach had disturbed it before it could secure a good grip on its victim for, as it flew across the road, the pheasant slipped from its grasp and fell heavily to the ground. As the hawk disappeared over a nearby knoll, I got out of the car and retrieved the dead pheasant which its captor had neatly decapitated preparatory to carrying it off. This is as near as I have ever come to the ancient sport of falconry.

Poultry, game birds, rabbits, and squirrels comprise the chief items of diet of this deadly winged destroyer. It ranges widely through North America.

THE DUCK HAWK

The duck hawk, or peregrine, of America is a close relative of the European peregrine falcon, the bird most often trained to kill ducks, partridges, and doves for hunters in olden times. It differs from the European falcon only in the coloration of its throat and breast.

Its size, about that of a crow, helps to identify this species, along with its dusky back, barred belly, and dark "mustaches." Its wings are long and pointed, its tail long and narrow. Its rapid wingbeat, unlike that of most other hawks, also serves to identify it.

These hawks range throughout North America, and were it not for the fact that their numbers have declined in recent years, they would comprise as great a threat to game birds as their relative the Cooper's hawk.

As it is, the duck hawk does very well. No bird is more efficiently designed for its role of killer. None flies faster than this winged thunderbolt, which spirals above its intended target and then dives in a sudden devastating strike. No evasive tactics on the part of the victim can avert its fate. Sometimes the duck hawk attacks with closed talons, delivering a blow that kills instantly. Smaller prey is snatched up in sharp, curved talons that stab the victim through and through.

All too often these victims include grouse, pheasants, and the larger songbirds. After their young are fledged, duck hawk families often move to coastal areas where waterfowl and shorebirds are plentiful.

The duck hawk's range includes most of North America, but civilization has encroached upon its nesting places, thereby considerably reducing its numbers and hence its depredations.

THE GOSHAWK

The goshawk is another killer, equal in fierceness and deadliness to the duck hawk. This is the largest of the American *Accipiters*, with an average length of twenty-four inches and a wingspread from forty to forty-seven inches. It is best identified in flight by its long tail and broad, rounded wings. Its distinguishing feature close up is a white stripe over the eye.

The goshawk is one of the most destructive of all hawks to game birds, poultry, and small mammals, and only the fact that it remains in its northern breeding grounds during the summer months prevents its depredations over most of the pheasant range from being greater than they are. Goshawks breed in the wooded regions of Canada and as far south as northern Michigan and northern New England, wintering south in Missouri and Virginia.

Most of the other hawks strike and, if they miss, go about their business —but not the goshawk. If its initial "stoop" misses its prey, it will follow the intended victim into the densest thicket, flush it into the open, and kill it forthwith. Few birds or mammals escape its persistent pursuit.

Sometimes it swallows its prey whole, but larger game birds and animals are torn into convenient bite-sized pieces. Its gluttonous appetite and rapid assimilation cause it to consume an inordinate amount of food daily. Indigestible matter is contracted in its stomach into pellets of fur, feathers, and bone which are regurgitated prior to further feeding.

The goshawk's fierceness is matched by its fearlessness. There are authenticated stories of hunger-driven goshawks diving upon crippled or dead game birds even as the hunter or his dog approaches to retrieve them.

THE PIGEON HAWK

The pigeon hawk receives its name not because it preys upon pigeons and doves (although it does), but rather because it somewhat resembles the pigeon both in body conformation and in flight. It also somewhat resembles the duck hawk, but is smaller. The best identifying marks are the slaty gray back and broad black bands on the tail of the male, and the female's dusky brown coloration.

Despite its miniature size, the pigeon hawk is highly destructive to birds, which comprise its principal fare. Fortunately for pheasants, it is a northern bird, breeding in northern Canada and seldom venturing south of northern California and northern Maine except in winter. Thus, it is seldom found in prime pheasant range during the breeding and nesting season. It attacks in the same manner as the duck and goshawk, and with equal ferocity.

SHARP-SHINNED HAWK

No list of killer hawks would be complete without the ubiquitous sharp-shinned hawk, along with the Cooper's hawk the most abundant and widely distributed of all. A rather small hawk about fourteen inches in length with a wingspread from twenty-two to twenty-eight inches, it can be identified by its long tail and short, rounded wings. The tail is square at the tip and slightly notched. Adults have slaty backs and chestnut-barred breasts.

This is one of the commonest of all hawks, and among the most destructive. The bulk of its food consists of songbirds, but it also takes its share of young poultry and game birds. Uttering shrill cries, this bird dives on its prey like the goshawk, striking birds in midair or pursuing them into thickets. Sharp-shinned hawks breed from Alaska and Newfoundland south to Panama.

THE OWLS

The hours of darkness bring no respite to song- and game birds, for dusk sets other winged marauders on the prowl, killers as deadly and silent as those that fly by day—the nocturnal family of owls.

Not all owls are destructive to game birds, and several are beneficial to man. Among the latter may be included the burrowing owl, the long-eared owl, the barn owl, the pygmy owl, the saw-whet owl, and the screech owl. Upon occasions, some of these members of the tribe may seize a young pheasant, but by far the major portion of their diet consists of rodents.

The three most serious offenders among the owls are the great horned owl, the barred owl, and the snowy owl. This infamous trio is enough to effect major inroads among game bird populations. By far the greatest menace is the great horned owl, a large bird about two feet in length with a five-foot wingspread. The conspicuous ear tufts or "horns" are the identifying marks of this large owl. The long-eared owl is somewhat similar but is much smaller, scarcely larger than a crow.

It is difficult to say much that is favorable about this rapacious killer, except that the outdoors would be a poorer place without the great horned owl's booming cries echoing through the night. It is one of the true voices of the wilderness. Anyone who has heard the deep-throated "hooo-hooo-hooo-hooo-hooo-o-o-o" of a hunting horned owl drifting across fields and woodlands is not likely to forget it. It is designed to strike terror to the heart of prey, causing it to start and thus reveal its presence. Sometimes it is varied by a rapid "hoo-hoo-hoo-hoo-hoo-hoo" and sometimes by a sudden, piercing shriek that can stand one's hair on end.

The barred owl is another good-sized bird, some twenty inches in length and with a wingspread of forty-five inches. Unlike the other owls, its eyes are brown. It can be identified by its round head, the crosswise barring of its breast, and the lengthwise streaking of its belly.

This is the gray brown owl of the deep woods but, unfortunately for pheasants, it frequently makes its home close to civilization where food in the form of rats, mice, poultry, and game birds is more plentiful.

Its hunting cry of "who-who-whooooo" sounds across the twilight fields as it takes to the air for a night of hunting. Like all owls, its plumage is remarkably soft, even to the wing primaries, which lack the stiffness found in other species of birds. This enables it to float silently and to swoop down upon its prey without a sound.

Like other owls, the barred owl regurgitates pellets of fur, feathers, and bone. These pellets found beneath a tree reveal the presence of a nesting site above. A common owl, the barred owl breeds from Newfoundland and northern Ontario to Colorado and south nearly to the Gulf of Mexico.

There are some who consider the snowy owl to be as fierce and destructive as the great horned owl, and this may well be so. However, as in the case of some of the hawks, its depredations in pheasant country are confined to winter months, for the rest of the year it breeds and dwells in the far north. Its presence south of the Canadian border in winter is irregular, depending upon the severity of the season in its native homeland.

This large owl, some two feet long and with a five-foot wingspread, is easily recognized by its snowy white body and its markings, especially in the male, of crosswise grayish bars around the shoulders and crown.

Snowy owls hunt by day as well as by night, seeking their prey among small mammals, ptarmigan, and ducks. Often they are seen perched motionless on stubs of trees, muskrat houses, and knolls. In winter they sometimes invade towns and cities. For several years a snowy owl spent the winter perched on a cornice of a bank in my hometown where it dined contentedly upon the pigeons that infested the town square. Not all snowy owls are so thoughtful. Others prefer to prey upon winter-bound grouse, pheasants, and rabbits, or to spend the cold months near coastal marshes where wildfowl abound.

OTHER PREDATORS

What has been said of foxes applies as well to coyotes in areas where their range overlaps that of pheasants. Bobcats, too, are accomplished killers of birds, but they generally keep to wilder lands than those frequented by pheasants, and hence find a place far down the list of the ringneck's predators. They do, however, share with the pheasants a predilection for swamps and, in certain areas, probably take their toll of birds.

It is the "tame" house cat more than its wild bobcat relative that poses a threat to pheasants. Farm cats, allowed to proliferate because of their supposed good offices in ridding barns and granaries of rats and mice, spend much of their time roaming the fields and woodlots in stealthy search of young birds and rabbits. The fledglings of ground-nesting birds, such as pheasants, are particularly vulnerable to these stealthy destroyers that often kill for fun.

A large black tomcat belonging to a farmer friend of mine last spring brought home four pheasant chicks in five days and escaped his richly merited fate because he was said to be a good mouser, and because he kept the farm liberally stocked with kittens.

Bluejays unquestionably take some toll of pheasant nests, but they too are more prone to rob the nests of songbirds. Snakes are fond of eggs and are undoubtedly responsible for the destruction of a number of nests each season, but almost certainly have no marked influence upon pheasant populations.

Opossums account for some loss of eggs. They have extended their range northward in recent years, but their numbers through pheasant range across the country are still not sizable enough to affect pheasant populations to any important degree.

Free-roaming dogs undoubtedly blunder upon nests and break them up upon occasion and certainly constitute a threat to nesting hens. Weasels, minks, and especially skunks destroy pheasant nests whenever they come upon them, but none of these pose a threat to pheasant supplies. All these species, however—crows, jays, snakes, opossums, dogs, weasels, minks, skunks—though no one of them is in itself a decisive factor, combined make very serious inroads into pheasant populations throughout the country.

As a matter of fact, these predators combined have been proven to be far more destructive than foxes, which have always been the favorite target of the "predators-must-go" faction.

To sum up, predators generally tend to prey on those species that are most available. A fox or an owl will seize a pheasant if it comes upon one, but opportunities vary widely with pheasant density and the type of cover in which they live. Predators as a group prefer to hunt more numerous and more easily captured prey in the form of mice, ground squirrels, and rabbits whose reproductive rates make them far more abundant than pheasants. In most cases, and in most areas, pheasants probably make up only a small portion of any individual predatory species' diet.

WEATHER

Animals, birds, and snakes are not the only destructive forces with which pheasants have to contend. Bad weather takes its toll. Spring floods, for example, can destroy nests and pheasant chicks on a far wider scale than can any predators.

Also, although the egg-laying instinct reveals itself in April, the nesting instinct is governed by weather. When spring comes late, hen pheasants lay eggs but do not make nests and incubate the eggs. Thus, they continue to lay extra eggs until they become broody, and the stress of this extra egg laying results in high mortality and poor pheasant years. Studies have shown a correlation with late springs and poor pheasant reproduction in Wisconsin and other states.

Even fair weather can be deleterious to pheasants. Prematurely hot days in May and June can adversely affect eggs. Air temperatures of 94 degrees result in nest temperatures of 112 degrees, which can cause damage to eggs.

The pheasant population in South Dakota fell from an estimated ten million birds in the fall of 1963 to about five million in the fall of 1964. April temperatures were normal, but May and June were abnormally hot with one ninety-four-degree day in May and six one-hundred-degree days in June.

Despite the bird's hardiness, sudden winter storms can take a great toll of pheasants. As many as 50 percent of the population can die of exposure and freezing in bad winters.
Courtesy, South Dakota Department of Game, Fish and Parks

It is generally supposed that winter causes the greatest mortality among pheasants, but actually more birds are lost between mid-May and August than at any other time. Rainy weather, hot weather, and droughts cause loss of cover and food and take a heavy toll of young and adult birds.

This is not to say that winter, too, is not a time of considerable mortality. Winter blizzards destroy numerous birds. Some starve to death, others become frozen to the ground, and still others suffocate when ice clogs their mouths and nasal passages.

And, finally, there is man—with his automobiles which annually kill thousands of birds along the highways, with his tractor-driven machinery that destroys untold thousands of nests, his fires that burn over nesting areas, destroying cover and eggs, with his pesticides and chemical fertilizers—man the habitat destroyer, man the poacher. All of these activities interrupt the scheme of pheasants' natural life, and have an effect on the levels of population at least as great as that of the other predators. Game biologists, for example, estimate that the number of nesting hens (not to mention incubating eggs) killed by high-speed haymowers is nearly as great as the numbers of cocks killed during hunting season.

With natural enemies, storms, heat, fire, poisons, and poaching, to say nothing of legal hunting, it is remarkable that pheasant populations even remain, much less continue to flourish on this earth.

Pheasant
Cover

Cover, food, and water are the basic requirements of all game birds and animals, including pheasants, and the first of these is almost as important as the others. For, without cover in which to nest and roost, pheasants would soon die from the effects of disease, predation, and exposure—no matter how plentiful their food supply might be. And in a sense the cover *is* the food, since it produces a large share of the pheasant's diet in the form of seeds, grasses, insects, nuts, and berries.

Where a fortuitous, or planned, combination of cover, food supplies, and water exists, pheasants will thrive; where one of these is lacking, pheasant populations will dwindle and disappear. A vivid illustration of suitable cover in pheasant ecology is provided by a look at what has happened to pheasant populations in South Dakota over the past thirty years.

First, though, we should go back somewhat further and trace the changing ecology of the region which brought about its emergence as a pheasant-producing state in the first place. A century and more ago the present state of South Dakota was a vast prairie, inhabited mostly by Indians and great herds of buffalo.

These herds, trampling and grazing as they roamed across the plains, had their own effect upon the land, which ended with their virtual disappearance because of their wholesale slaughter for meat and hides. With their passing, the face of the grasslands changed and became further altered as settlers moved in to plow and cultivate the prairie.

These changes created a new habitat for sharp-tailed grouse and prairie chickens which flourished in great numbers until after the turn of the century.

As more settlers moved into South Dakota and agriculture intensified, native grouse and prairie chicken populations declined through loss of habitat. But the same agricultural practices which sounded the death knell of these species created ideal conditions for ring-necked pheasants, which were introduced into the state between 1914 and 1917 to take the place of disappearing grouse and prairie chickens.

Pheasants found South Dakota's sloughs and grainfields almost perfect habitat. In fact, they thrived to such an extent that game management personnel were kept busy during those early years moving burgeoning flocks of pheasants to every suitable part of the state. The farming country of eastern South Dakota, especially, proved to be ideal habitat. It produced pheasants in astronomical numbers.

By the early 1940s South Dakota could boast, without challenge, of having the largest pheasant population of any state in the Union. Accurate records were not kept at that time, but some estimates place the number of pheasants at 30 million birds; certainly it was well over 15 million.

Then in three short years featuring cold springs and resultant poor hatches, the population plummeted by 1947 to 7 million birds. During the next fifteen years, pheasant populations rose and fell in a series of three-year cycles in which two good years were followed by a poor one. At the end of this period, the population dropped in 1962 from 11 million to 10.2 million birds.

Instead of gaining in 1963, however, it dropped further to 10 million and in 1964 plummeted to 5.1 million, *a loss of almost 50 percent!* By 1966 the pheasant population stood at 2.2 million birds. Since then it has risen to 4.5 million in 1973, still far from the abundance of the 1940s.

This long and severe decline cannot be traced entirely to diminution of cover. Weather, disease, and predation also played their roles. But directly or indirectly, the destruction of cover has been the chief factor in the decline and in preventing populations from rebounding to their former levels.

The pheasant population explosion of the 1940s coincided with World War II, when farm machinery was hard to come by, gasoline was rationed, and farm labor scarce. As a result, dense cover spread over untended fields and ungrazed range, and the pheasants spread with it.

With the war's end, intensive agriculture resumed. More land was placed under cultivation, more livestock grazed the range, and alfalfa took the place of small grains. The sunflower and ragweed jungles of the war years disappeared before the new clean-farming practices, aided by newly designed farm machinery and new herbicides. Fall plowing became more common, leaving many winter fields denuded of cover.

Pheasant populations might have begun to decline earlier than 1963 as a result of these changes, had it not been for the soil bank program of the late 1950s and early '60s. During that period some two million acres of good farmland—about 10 percent of the state's crop land—were planted to grasses and legumes, in order to reduce crop surpluses. No grazing or haying were permitted on soil bank acreage.

As a result, pheasant populations actually increased during these years, from 7.5 million to over 10 million birds. Thus, the soil bank quite unintentionally became a large-scale experiment that proved the value of cover to pheasants and the fact that pheasant populations will expand as available cover increases.

Then in the summer of 1964 a severe drought visited the pheasant range of South Dakota, producing an agricultural emergency. To combat its effects, thousands of soil bank acres were mowed and grazed to provide feed for starving livestock. With the consequent loss of cover, the pheasant population in that one year fell from 11 million to 5.1 million birds and, as we have seen, was destined to fall much lower.

The slight gain of the past few years from a low of 2.2 million to 4.5 million birds has come about in part from the increase in irrigation projects in South Dakota. Weed-grown irrigation ditches have created more habitat and have replaced to an extent some of the cover lost by changes in land use and clean farming. However, it seems doubtful that the huge populations of the 1940s will ever be seen again in South Dakota, unless unforeseen circumstances bring about a return of the cover conditions which prevailed in those years—a possibility that seems remote.

So, when we talk about pheasant cover, we are speaking in general terms of several specific needs, including nesting cover, escape and travel cover, roosting cover, and winter cover. All of these types of cover must be located within a one-and-a-half-mile radius, the average range of individual pheasants. If one or more of these various types of cover are destroyed, pheasant populations in the area will suffer.

If nesting cover is reduced, hens' nests will be concentrated in a smaller area, making them easier for predators to find. If cover is thin, eggs are that much more vulnerable to heat, cold, and rain. When escape and travel covers are removed by clean farming, pheasants' roaming tendencies will be limited and they will become easier for predators to locate. And when corn is cut for silage, fields are plowed in the fall, and weeds are eradicated by herbicides, fewer pheasants will be able to survive the ensuing winter.

SCOUTING THE COVER

From this general discussion of cover as it affects pheasant populations as a whole, let's turn to consider cover as it relates to the hunting of individual pheasants. This subject, of course, can become somewhat complicated by the fact that in many states today the pheasant's natural selection of cover is influenced by stocking programs. In other words, game farm personnel frequently liberate pheasants in areas the pheasants would never choose for themselves.

One time, for example, I came upon a state truck whose driver was busy releasing pheasants at the edge of a wide, mowed field with no cover in sight. To me, it appeared that he was more interested in getting home to supper than in providing suitable habitat for his newly liberated birds. However, those that survive for two or three days soon find cover adequate for their needs. Thus, in talking about hunting covers here, the emphasis will be upon those types chosen by the birds themselves.

The serious pheasant gunner should begin his hunting activities in the spring—not with a gun, of course, and not necessarily with a dog. Rather, the hunting should be done with one's eyes. This kind of hunting—perhaps scouting is a better word—is valuable whether it is carried on in old, familiar gunning territory or in new and strange surroundings.

Each spring, shortly after the snow has left the ground, I make it a point to visit my favorite pheasant-shooting areas. There are several things I want to find out: what, if any, changes the winter has brought, the general look of the landscape, and indications of what the coming summer might be like.

One change to look for today, unfortunately, is the conversion of a perfectly good pheasant swale into a shopping plaza or real estate development. Last spring I visited a former corn piece bordered by brushy woodlands which had been a favorite haunt of mine, and of pheasants, for many years. On this April day I found hard-topped roads winding about the muddy field with building lots laid out and marked by numbers. Some already bore wooden signs that said SOLD. And so came to an end another happy hunting ground.

If a field has, however, escaped the bulldozers so far, there are a number of things it can tell you in the spring. I look first to see whether leftover vegetation is sparse or heavy. If the latter, it means good nesting cover and a better source of food until new vegetation appears to take its place.

Burned-over fields are not a good omen. For, even though the burning may be done before nesting season, it is inevitably going to destroy valuable

A farmer burned over his spring field—and this crop of pheasants. Courtesy, South Dakota Department of Fish, Game and Parks

cover and especially if the fields are burned right to the edges, leaving no grown-up fencerows. Farmers plowing fields can, however, be a good sign, especially if the fields are soon to be planted in corn, tomatoes, potatoes, or any of the other crops pheasants enjoy. Fields designed to grow hay are good, too, for they will provide nesting, resting, and escape cover. Fields left fallow to grow up in weeds and brambles are best of all, for they will attract birds to roost and feed. All these indications of what the summer holds in store are valuable forecasters of the potential hunting possibilities for autumn.

From these generalities I turn to more specific considerations. If I hear several cock pheasants crowing, I know that the population is high and that there will be a good number of nests secreted in roadside brush, tangled fields, and woodland edges. If I hear only one rooster or none, I know that winter has taken a toll and the quality of the hunting will depend in part on the efforts of the game farm truck.

I keep a lookout, of course, for the birds themselves, and sometimes flush a cock and several hens from thin spring cover. I also look and listen for the sight and sound of predators. The tracks of a raccoon or mink along the muddy bank of a swollen brook mean danger for nesting pheasants and their eggs. A new fox den dug into the base of a wooded knoll means trouble ahead for the pheasants that dwell in this swale. So does a Cooper's hawk sitting motionless on a limb of a dead tree, as does the flock of crows cawing above the pines bordering the swale.

In wandering through the area I look for other things. Have the fence-rows along the muddy back road been left uncut? Is the brush-choked escape ravine that leads to the swamp still intact? All these things give an overall picture of how the area has come through the winter and what the future may hold.

But much can happen between April and October—even another shopping center—and so, in order to keep abreast of the developing situation, it is necessary to make several preseason trips to your pheasant range, one every month or so.

By June the promise of spring will have further unfolded. By now new vegetation will have grown up to cover the brown landscape of early spring. Fields and fencerows, swamps and woodlands—all will be thick with new foliage, and by now you can get a pretty good idea as to whether or not this is going to be a season of rank, heavy growth. Also, at this time of year you will know what was planted in those fields that were being plowed in April. Young corn stands green across one of them, potato vines rise in another, and beet tops redden in still another.

Grass in the mowings is almost knee-high by June and cattails thrust brown heads above the swamps. In the tall grass, at the edge of dusty roadsides, by the edges of woods, and in low dingles hen pheasants are on their nests. Already some broods have hatched and, if you are lucky, you may see a handful of chicks following their mother into a patch of clover.

On sunny slopes you will see the worn depressions in the ground which mark the loafing and dusting spots of pheasants during midday. And in your wanderings you may come upon a little heap of feathers where some predator has made its kill.

A later trip in midsummer will reveal your swale much as it will look in fall before the first hard frosts. The corn is in silk now with ears formed on the stalks. Potato vines are high and thick with white blossoms. Fields of wheat stubble lie yellow in the sun. Fencerows are choked with dense vegetation and brush, and weed-grown fields have turned to tangled jungles.

Grass rises waist-high in the swamps, and the bordering woods are dark and green and shady. Fields have now been mowed and the rowan is ankle-deep. Insects hop and fly and buzz across the fields, and fruit and berries are ripening.

By now you should have a very good idea of what the fall will be like —heavy cover or light, dry swamps or wet, good apple year or no apples, abundant or scarce acorns and beechnuts. All this, with your knowledge of the location and condition of corn and potato fields, weed fields, wheat fields, milo, alfalfa, and hay will give you a pretty good idea of where to look for birds during the open season. And a good bird dog, at this time of year when the young are on the wing, will also give you some indication of how many native birds are going to be using these covers.

HUNTING THE COVER

And so, at last, comes the hunting season. The smart pheasant gunner will be abroad early, as early as gunning is permitted by law, for pheasants begin moving from their roosts with the first faint streaks of dawn. Often they walk from roosting to feeding grounds, but they may fly, depending upon the distance and probably on certain other factors known only to themselves.

The early gunner who has done his homework and knows where pheasant roosting and feeding areas are located can often intercept a bird on its way to breakfast. Fencerows, brushy ravines, and other travel lanes are good places to hunt at this time of morning.

Last October on opening day I drove to a favorite cover that I had scouted several times since spring. There were already several cars parked beside the swale, although it was not yet light. To lessen the competition somewhat, I drove around to the other side of the field and left my car at the entrance to a wood road. I knew that beyond the woods a fencerow led from a swamp to a harvested cornfield, and I decided to start my hunt in this area. To get there I had to walk about a half mile and by the time I arrived at my destination it would be legal shooting time.

Dawn whitened the east as I walked silently down the wood road. Faint stirrings rustled around me as the woods gradually awakened. A squirrel scuttered across a little clearing and whisked to the top of a nearby maple. A bluejay screamed at my approach and crows cawed above the pines.

The first lavender banners of sunrise showed in the sky as I emerged from the trees and headed for the fencerow. My choice proved to be a good one. Released from his lead, my Brit bounded away at full speed, but before he had gone a hundred feet he put on the brakes, wheeled, and egg walked to a point.

As I came up, he broke, moved stealthily ahead again ... again ... and froze. When I walked into the tangled grass, a cock pheasant clattered into the air. For a second it hung silhouetted against the sunrise sky and then plummeted at the blast of my over-and-under. The season was ten minutes old.

I'm not always as fortunate as this by any means, but my preseason scouting trips had given me an idea of where a bird might be—and this time he was.

After hunting along the birds' travel corridors, the next places to hunt are the feeding grounds where pheasants spend the first several hours of the morning. Their choice of feeding areas is influenced by several factors: the

Hunting grassy, open slopes where pheasants spend the afternoon sunning and dusting . . .

. . . pays off. Photos by author

stage of the season, the availability of various types of food, the presence or absence of natural enemies in certain feeding places, and their own individual choice of fare.

Again, the gunner who knows what kinds of food are available, and where, has the edge over the man who is hunting for pheasant feeding grounds as well as pheasants. Cornfields are always a good bet, for grain is a favorite item of pheasant diet and is easy for them to come by.

If the corn has been cut, the birds will seldom try to hide in the open field when danger threatens but, instead, will run into the nearest adjacent cover. That is why cornfields bordered by woodlots or grown-up fields are ideal places to hunt during feeding periods.

Uncut corn is another matter. Pheasants can and do hide in fields of uncut corn and will lead dogs and hunters a frustrating chase in these surroundings. About the only practical way to hunt these fields is for several hunters to drive the birds through the corn toward other hunters standing at the end of the field. Even then, a number of birds will run out on either side.

In good apple years, orchards are apt to be happy hunting grounds, especially when there are windfalls lying under the trees. The tangled grass found in most orchards also provides excellent hiding places. Orchards should be thoroughly hunted in good apple years. And don't neglect wetlands—pheasants don't!

Grown-up weed fields are another good bet, combining as they do both food and safety from enemies. When the fields contain bramble tangles, as they often do, these are places to investigate carefully. Weed fields are generally better hunting grounds later in the season after heavy frosts have destroyed other foods. When crops such as grain, potatoes, tomatoes, or apples are available, they will attract the majority of birds.

Late in the season, you will also often find pheasants in wooded areas where acorns and beechnuts are available. And, as a matter of fact, smart pheasant cocks will often make their way to dense wooded areas as soon as the guns begin to boom.

I remember one day when I was hunting grouse in a rather thick grown-up woods behind an abandoned farmhouse. When my companion's setter went on point, we naturally thought he had pinned a grouse, although in the area where we were hunting, few grouse waited around to be pinned. When the dog broke and trailed for some distance, we supposed the grouse was running and waited momentarily for the explosion of wings ahead. The trail finally ended in a thick clump of ferns, and when my companion walked in a cock pheasant cackled into the air instead of a grouse.

My companion was so startled that he missed the bird clean with his first barrel, but managed to connect with the second. This cock was a huge one with long, heavy spurs—one that had been around long enough to have learned that guns mean trouble. The interesting thing was that the nearest conventional pheasant cover was in the valley a good mile or more away.

Especially in the late season, then, or in areas of heavy hunting pressure, don't pass up thickly wooded areas. They often hold one or more crafty cocks well worth bagging. Gun-wise late season birds will often retreat to cover in the very center of farm sections, as far as possible from their favored roadside covers.

In the West and Midwest, pheasants have learned to accept alfalfa and soybeans, instead of seeds, as their main diet. So during the feeding periods they'll be in or near the planted fields; afterwards they can be found in adjacent low-lying areas. Wary birds may retreat to sunny hillsides to rest and dust, in safety.

Pheasants remain in the feeding covers from dawn until about midmorning. From then until early afternoon these areas will be deserted. Yet many gunners spend time and energy hunting these places long after the pheasants have left them and before they return for the afternoon feeding period. Instead of wasting time hunting feeding areas, the knowledgeable gunner will turn his attention to areas where pheasants spend the midday hours loafing, dusting, and digesting their morning meal—areas that he knows from his earlier scouting expeditions.

Prime among these places are sunny slopes covered with some sort of fairly sparse vegetation in the form of shrubs, grasses, or small conifers. You can often tell them by the round dusting places scattered here and there. These places should be approached cautiously and as quietly as possible.

Actually, silence is an important ingredient of all pheasant hunting. The slam of a car door, even the sound of voices, is often enough to send pheasants scurrying for cover. Therefore, it's a good idea to be as quiet as possible, and especially in approaching resting cover on clear, quiet days.

Old, grown-up gravel pits are other favorite resting spots for pheasants at noonday. If there is such a place in your pheasant-hunting territory, mark it well and plan to explore it during the resting period. Other good places to investigate are grown-up ditch banks and wide hedgerows that afford exposure to the sun.

And again, sometimes mid- or late-season birds spend their rest periods in unlikely places, often in small niches of cover in relatively open land away from normal resting areas.

I well recall an occasion when I hunted through a weedy field to a deserted gravel pit at the far end. There were no birds around the pit, and I was about to continue on to a hillside knoll which I knew pheasants were accustomed to frequent at midday. At that point, however, my Brit made a wide cast across the field and suddenly caught scent.

Circling and zigzagging toward a patch of brambles hardly six feet wide, then slowing his pace, he moved cautiously forward to a staunch point. It seemed incredible that there could be a bird in so small a space, but his whole tense attitude said "Pheasants!"

I walked toward the bramble patch and just as I reached the dog, not one

In the West, wary pheasants sometimes move into side pockets along the edges of coulees for safety during the midday resting period. Courtesy, Larry Mueller

but *two* cock pheasants flushed cackling out of the brush. I already had one pheasant in my game pocket and the daily limit in my state is two, so I shot one and then was forced to watch the other sail away across the field, contenting myself with putting the gun muzzles on him and saying "bang" in a loud voice. It was a perfect chance for a double—but then it isn't inconceivable that I might have missed.

Two or three hours before dusk, the birds begin their return to the feeding grounds to fill their crops before going to roost. Again, at this time of day they can often be intercepted along travel corridors or flushed to the gun from the orchards, grainfields, and other places which were productive during the earlier morning feeding period.

At the end of the day a visit to known roosting grounds in grown-up fields, swamps, or brushy pastures may well complete the hunter's bag. Wheat stubble is a favorite roosting place, and many a bird has been shot in this sort of cover in the late afternoon.

Hunting any type of cover on very windy days, it's a good idea (especially for the dogless hunter) to hunt into the wind, so that the birds have less chance of hearing your approach. And on rainy and wet days, pheasants have a tendency to sit tighter than on dry days. Sometimes in heavy rains it is almost necessary to kick them into the air to make them fly.

Remember, too, that a pheasant's eyesight is very sharp, and once he sights a possible enemy, he waits not upon the manner of his going. I have frequently seen running pheasants gain ground on a trailing dog. They will keep on running until the cover gives out, so if you hunt toward a break in cover, or from heavier cover into thinner, running birds will often flush more readily. Some, of course, will just keep on running, but that's one of the reasons pheasants are so hard to come by and pheasant hunting so fascinating a sport.

Bags like this are the reward of a well-planned hunt, based on knowledge of the cover and practiced wing shooting. Photo by author

*Pheasants were here: as long as they can reach their food supplies, they will survive **normal** snowfalls.* Courtesy, South Dakota Department of Fish, Game and Parks

To round out the year—and your knowledge of pheasant cover—it is interesting once in a while to walk the winter fields after the gunning season has ended. Look for pheasant tracks in the new snow, and also for those of predators on the hunt. Roam the feeding areas, the roosting covers, and the resting spots, noting where weed seeds lift above the snow where mounded brush and last year's matted vegetation give shelter from storms.

Your observations will give you a new respect for these hardy birds, surviving in the face of ice and snow and cold, subsisting on whatever they can find as they wait for another spring. Sometimes you will see them, silhouetted against the winter whiteness, bands of feeding hens in a sheltered gully or a solitary cock following along a drifted fencerow.

If they have adequate cover, they will make it through the winter, and perhaps provide you with yet another season of fine sport.

Pheasant Shooting

As every gunner knows, there is a considerable difference between pheasant hunting and pheasant *shooting*. All too often, a hunter does a flawless job right up to the point where his quarry bursts cackling from a clump of weeds, only to see his pheasant dinner plane away across the fields unscathed. Pheasant shooting can be a very humbling sport.

First, of course, you have to find your bird—the hunting part of the business. But a successful gunner must know not only *where* but also *how* to hunt pheasants, and hopefully how to shoot them when they flush.

HUNTING WITHOUT A DOG

Many gunners, for a variety of reasons, hunt pheasants without a dog—and successfully, too. But hunting without a dog calls for techniques some-

Hunting good early-season cover: weedy fields that provide pheasants with both food and cover. Photo by author

what different from those employed by hunters with dogs.

Probably the most important rule for the dogless hunter to keep in mind is to hunt SLOWLY, pausing every few feet to listen and look around. This cannot be overemphasized. For, as we have seen, as soon as a pheasant becomes aware of the presence of an enemy, he is apt to begin a rapid sneak to put as much territory as possible between himself and the danger. Without a dog, you are not going to be able to trail him, and so you are going to have few opportunities to bag running birds.

The pheasants that *are* going to end up in your game bag are the ones that you come upon before they are aware of you—when a wind covers your approach or soft ground enables you to move silently—and those that you come upon in cover that they consider adequate to conceal themselves in safety. And often the pheasant is right, depending to a large degree upon the skills of the hunter.

Far too many pheasant hunters move through the cover at a pace more suited for a brisk constitutional than for flushing birds. A pheasant crouched beneath a briar tangle is completely safe as long as he remains motionless for the few seconds it takes such hunters to pass him by and move out of range.

It's a far different situation for the pheasant when the hunter approaches slowly and pauses frequently. John Pheasant, hiding beneath that same bramble tangle, thinks to himself, "Danger! But it isn't coming very fast. There's still time to run. Or shall I hide here? Now he's stopped—what shall I do? There he goes. I guess he didn't see me. Oh oh! He's stopped again. Maybe he does see me. I'd better get the hell out of here!" Perhaps these aren't his exact thought processes, but this is effectively what happens. And, hopefully, he flushes into the path of a well-aimed charge of number 6 shot.

It's also a good idea to walk a zigzag course. This enables you to cover an area more fully than on a straight course.

One day when I was hunting without a dog, I saw another gunner roam through a grown-up field that I had planned to hunt. He was moving at a leisurely pace, but I noticed that he kept to the middle of the field, which was rather narrow but was bordered by brush on both sides. I decided that he was leaving quite a lot of territory untouched so, after a pipe beside the car, I wandered into the same field, moving in a zigzag pattern from one side to the other.

Perhaps the hunter who had preceded me had scared a pheasant into taking refuge in the thick brush at the right side of the field. Anyway, one was there and, as I paused beside a weedy thicket, he suddenly burst into the air for an easy crossing shot.

If there are two hunters working together, this type of zigzag course will enable them to cover the same area in half the time. Had I had a companion with me in the foregoing situation, we would both have started at the same end of the field. One of us would have zigzagged back and forth from midfield to the right side and the other from midfield to the left side. By moving *slowly* we would have had a good chance to intercept any hiding birds. Not only is zigzagging effective for tight-lying birds, but it also counters the "run-ahead, circle, and run-back" tactic of cock birds.

HUNTING FENCEROWS

Fencerows are prime areas for the man hunting without a dog, since the cover is apt to be narrow and bordered by open fields. Here again, the way to make haste is slowly. If you walk rapidly, your quarry is all too apt to run ahead of you and flush far out of range. If you move slowly, with frequent pauses, the bird will be more likely to sneak along at a moderate pace or to sit tight in some particularly brushy spot. You should pause and investigate these thick places thoroughly.

The time to be especially alert is when you approach the end of the row. For if there is a bird running ahead of you, now is the time he is most likely to flush. You might even accelerate your pace for the final fifty feet or so in order to push him into the air. If the end of the fencerow forms a corner with another, the bird may flush, or he may turn the corner and follow the new row.

One day I saw a pheasant run across the corner of a harvested cornfield into a fencerow. I wasn't sure whether he had seen me or not, but I began moving slowly along the brushy row toward the spot where he had entered it. I came to the end of it without a flush, so I continued along another row which joined the first one at right angles. When I came to the end of that row, I decided that either the bird had run into some adjacent cover or that I had passed him by.

It was late in the day, so I headed back toward the car, following another fencerow that bordered a third side of the cornfield. It was when I came nearly to the end of that row that a cock pheasant rocketed up out of the brush and flew straight away from me. At the blast of my shotgun he crumpled and came down. Of course, I can't be sure that this was the same bird I had seen previously, but I feel strongly that it was, and that he had run around three sides of the field before flushing.

Two men can hunt a fencerow even better than one. One way is to take opposite sides, especially if it is a wide, brushy fencerow, and move along abreast. This will help prevent birds from running out to one side or the other as they occasionally do, especially if there is cover nearby.

Another method is for one man to hunt from one end of the row while the second hunts from the other. This tactic prevents birds from running out at either end and usually assures a shot. However, both men must be alert to see that no birds escape to one side or the other. And even more important, as the partners draw together, both must know who is to take the shot, if any.

This arrangement must be decided ahead of time. For example, any birds on the right-hand side belong to the gunner on that side, any on the left to his companion. On doubles each man takes the nearer bird and so on.

To execute this hunt successfully and safely, the gunners must be confident of each other's gun-handling abilities and good judgment. An alternative method is for one man to stand at one end of the row while his companion hunts from the other end, but with a trusted companion, I like the first method better.

DRIVING A FIELD

Something of the same sort of technique is often used by a group of hunters in driving fields, an especially popular hunting method in the grain belt states. Three gunners are stationed at one end of a standing cornfield to wait while their companions drive their car to the other end of the field.

Two of these latter hunters take up positions at each corner of the field where the cornstalks are bordered by thickets of ragweed, and the third midway between them. These men are "stoppers" or "blockers." Before crouching to hide themselves, one of them waves his cap as a signal to the men at the far end of the field that the stoppers are ready.

Spaced fifteen to twenty corn rows apart, the drivers now begin a slow advance among the stalks, guns ready for action. Almost immediately, a gaudy cock bird cackles up from the shoulder-high corn near one of the drivers and angles across his path, his iridescent colors shining in the sun. At a blast of the gun the bird sags and plumps down amid the standing corn.

As the drive continues, three hens flush ahead of the right-hand gunner and split away to either side. All three present easy shots but no one fires, though the law allows one hen in the bag in this state. These hunters prefer cock birds.

The gunners move on, noting the ears of yellow corn hanging from the stalks or strewn upon the ground, most of them stripped clean by pheasants. Tracks and droppings show everywhere in the dusty soil, and there should be a number of birds sneaking along ahead of the drive.

Tension mounts as the drive nears the end of the field. Hearts beat faster and fingers slide nervously toward safety catches. The big moment is at hand.

It comes with breathtaking suddenness. The gunner in the middle pushes through a tangle of downed cornstalks and, as if at a signal, a cock bird clatters up ten yards ahead. As it crumples at the gunner's shot, a dozen birds rocket out of the corn with others close behind them. The air is filled with cackles, beating wings, and gunfire. As the hunters fumble to reload, pheasants continue to flush on all sides, the survivors planing away against the blue prairie sky. That's a typical midwestern pheasant hunt.

In a booklet called "The Ring-necked Pheasant," game biologist John

Madson describes several drive techniques which hunting parties without dogs can use both in standing corn and in large grass fields. The basic strategy of this kind of hunting, Madson says, is to cover as much field as possible without allowing the birds to double back through the line of drivers, or lie tight while they walk by. A zigzag course works best, but if the drivers walk straight down the field they should not be separated by more than thirty feet. And by driving in a shallow V pattern, with the open end of the V toward the blockers, pheasants may be prevented from escaping at the sides of the line.

Furthermore, hunters should avoid downwind drives. The pheasants will always be well aware of the locations of the upwind drivers, and the birds' chances of finding an opening or of lying tight will be that much better. In crosswind drives, birds that flush before the blockers will probably flush into the wind and then quarter downwind. Madson recommends that one gunner be stationed on the downwind side, fifty to sixty yards ahead of the rest of the drivers, to catch these birds.

Once again, silence can be an important factor, even in this kind of a hunt. Blockers should be quiet and inconspicuous, especially in dry, late-season cover. Madson even cautions that blockers not be stationed until the drivers are in position, as awareness of hunters may spread among the pheasants very quickly, and they will tend to sift out of the sides of the field. If there is a grass or slough area at one end or corner of the field, Madson suggests the birds be worked toward those places. They'll hold longer there and allow more time for the blockers to get into position for the final push.

When hunting without a dog it's my personal preference to concentrate on fencerows and small brushy or weed-grown areas of the sort that I can cover thoroughly by myself. I leave the big fields, swamps, and swales for hunting with a dog. However, I never pass up a field, orchard, or swamp on the route of my hunt.

I recall one time passing through a large, swampy field with an alder-fringed brook winding through its center. I was on my way to a small, brushy border beyond, but since the field lay in my path, I hunted through it carefully.

At the far end I noticed a hunter and his setter following along the brook toward me. I changed my course to the brushy edge of the field, to get out of their way. As I skirted the brush, a cock pheasant suddenly jumped, about six feet ahead of me. I was so startled by the sudden, cackling explosion that I missed the bird with the first barrel. But I managed to bring him down with the second as he sailed toward the center of the field.

With the first snows of winter, real opportunities arise in all kinds of cover for the dogless hunter. After a new snow, it's possible actually to track pheasants as they go about their business of feeding and resting. A cock pheasant's trail will usually be marked by a characteristic line between the footprints made by the dragging tail. Often they can be trailed right into

Cock pheasants are easily trailed in new snow: their dragging tail feathers leave a telltale line between their tracks. Courtesy, South Dakota Department of Fish, Game and Parks

brushy cover from which they can be flushed and shot. It's a sport that provides a great deal of fun and excitement, even when uncrowned by success.

After light snows, a good place to look for pheasants is in small weed patches adjacent to grainfields. Shelter belts are also productive places to hunt at this time of year. Following heavy snowstorms, pheasants have a tendency to travel shorter distances and, when trailed, to take refuge in thick, brushy hiding places. Occasionally, you will see the long tails of cock birds protruding from snow-covered weed clumps or fireweed plants.

HUNTING WITH A DOG

Hunting pheasants without a dog is a good sport, and thousands of birds are bagged annually by dogless hunters. But there is no denying the fact that hunters with dogs find more pheasants, usually get better shots at those they

This pointer held his ground until his hunter could join him; that was too much for the bird, and up he went. Judging from the relaxed stance of this shooter—the feet are at the proper right-angle to the line of fire—the bird will probably come down as well. Courtesy, Frank Woolner

find, and certainly lose far fewer crippled birds. Added to all these advantages is the heartwarming pleasure and excitement of watching a good bird dog doing what he loves to do best.

And finally, the gunner with a dog has wider opportunities. For not only can he hunt the fencerows, weed patches, and other small covers suited to the man without a dog, but he can also hunt wide fields, swamps, and swales with confidence that if there are any birds in these areas, his dog is probably going to find them.

Pheasant hunting with a dog, especially in the East, often takes on many of the characteristics of an old-fashioned fox hunt. Pheasants will run across brooks—or even swim if necessary—they will circle, backtrack, dodge, twist, and if all else fails, finally fly. More than once I have followed my Brit across a weed field, through a woodlot, and deep into a swamp before he finally caught up to a fast-pacing rooster.

On one occasion, hunting with a friend and his beagle Tim, the fox-hunt analogy became startlingly real. We were hunting a harvested cornfield, bordered by a narrow strip of woods which in turn was bordered by railroad tracks. On several earlier occasions, birds had flown from this field to safety across the tracks, and so to circumvent this maneuver I was walking along the railroad enbankment while my companion and Tim combed the field.

I had just reached a point near the end of the field where a small brook wound through a brushy ravine to flow through a culvert beneath the embankment. All at once I heard Tim's voice—not the confident, long-drawn note that signifies a rabbit on the run, but a sort of questing yelp that he reserves for pheasants. The game was afoot! I gripped my gun tighter and peered anxiously up the alder-choked ravine.

The yelps continued, obviously moving in my direction. As I slid the safety off, I felt as I had on other occasions, standing at a barway on a hillside pasture listening tensely as a chorus of foxhound music swelled. Nearer and nearer came the sound of Tim's eager yelping and then I saw him, a glimmer of white among the alders. I raised my gun and waited for the flush.

Now I could see Tim more plainly, vacuuming the ground as he followed along the brook. The suspense grew as he approached—but to my amazement, there was no flush. Instead, Tim yelped his way to the embankment and disappeared inside the culvert. Somehow, that bird had run along the brook without a sound or a glimpse and, instead of flying, had followed it through the culvert! As I helplessly pondered these matters, Tim's yelps turned suddenly to muffled sounds of anguish. I scrambled down the sandy embankment to find him stuck in the culvert, just as his owner appeared upon the scene.

"What happened?" he wanted to know.

"The bird ran through the culvert and now your dog is stuck in it," I explained.

Lying on our bellies in mud, we managed to extricate Tim. As we worked at it, a crowing sound came from deep in the heart of the swamp beyond —a definitely sneering sort of crow.

Not all hunts end in such embarrassing contretemps, of course, but even *with* a dog you'll have your work cut out for you, trying to bag the seasoned bird.

WOUNDED BIRDS

Locating a killed pheasant usually poses little difficulty for man or dog, except in the thickest cover. Pheasants seem to lose their protective coloration when they fall to the ground cleanly killed and lie sprawled with outspread wings upon the grass or brush. Finding wounded or crippled birds, however, is quite another matter.

Pheasants are tough, hardy birds and can carry off an astonishing amount of lead if they're not hit in a vital area. An old pheasant gunner of my acquaintance used to declare that "the shot is just to bring 'em down so's you can wring their goddamned necks." His cynical comment contains elements of truth.

Even a mortally wounded pheasant will frequently fly for several hundred yards before crumpling. A hunting companion of mine once shot a cock bird and, for good measure, rapped its head against a rock before placing it in the trunk of his car. When he opened the trunk at home the pheasant flew out and disappeared over the rooftop of his house. And I recall one day when I shot a bird at close range. A few feathers flew, and so did the bird, without even flinching. I watched him plane away into a distant swamp and felt sure that he was only slightly wounded. Twenty minutes or so later, when I reached the edge of the swamp, my dog pointed and then lunged in and picked up my bird, which was stone dead. He had flown at least a half mile with his lungs torn by shot.

Now these are hard-hit pheasants, a number of which, regrettably, are never recovered. Wing-tipped or otherwise slightly wounded birds are even harder to retrieve. No fast sneak ahead of a dog with them. They will run like racehorses. Anyone who has ever seen a wing-tipped cock sprint across an open field must gain a new respect for his speed afoot. Without a good retriever he is almost certain to escape and end up as food for some predator.

I wing-tipped a bird one day—and apparently stunned him as well, for he came down in a heap. But when I got to the spot where he had landed he was gone, and my dog, after a brief cast about the area, took off at a gallop toward a nearby woods. At least five minutes went by before he returned, lugging the still-flapping pheasant in his jaws.

Experiences like these point up the importance of mastering the art—or craft, if you will—of wing shooting. No one, not even an expert, can score clean kills on every bird they shoot at. But the number of crippled and lost birds will decline sharply as the gunner's shooting skill increases.

PHEASANT SHOOTING RANGE

The chief cause of wounding and crippling—as well as complete misses —is shooting birds out of effective range. Pheasants, being large birds, are apt to appear nearer than they actually are. And hunters are more prone to shoot at out-of-range pheasants than at grouse or woodcock, for example, because pheasants are more often flushed in open cover where they can be seen at greater distances. An inexperienced hunter whom I took afield one day shot at a cock pheasant that rose beside a fence post and missed with both barrels.

"I don't see how I could have done that," he complained disconsolately. "I thought I was right on him."

"And how far off did you think he was?"

"About thirty yards or so," he replied promptly.

"Let's see," I suggested.

We paced off the distance from where he stood to the fence post and found it to be sixty-three yards, much too great a range for the 12-gauge gun and number 7½ shot he was using—even if he had fired the instant the bird flushed. Actually, it had flown eight or nine feet—another three yards —before my companion shot. For an average 12-gauge shotgun and ordinary loads, forty yards is extreme range for an improved cylinder barrel and is too far for outgoing pheasants.

It's helpful to learn to estimate a distance of forty yards fairly accurately. Set up a mark in your backyard and pace off forty yards. Or guess at forty-yard distances and correct your guesstimate by measurements. After a while you will have a good idea of this distance, and even then you should err on the right side by keeping well inside it when shooting at pheasants, especially with lighter-gauge guns. The man who brags about his successful long shots never tells you about the far larger number of birds he wounds —or misses.

In order to get more shots within range, it is important to stay as close as possible to a trailing dog and to get to a pointing dog fast. If you don't, the bird is apt to run again and ultimately to flush out of range. And when you walk in to flush, do so quickly and unhesitatingly, or again the bird will sneak away even as you approach.

SHOOTING AT PHEASANTS

Pheasants are not really difficult to hit. I have this upon the word of experts, of which group I am on the waiting list. They say that a good shot hunting with a dog should bag 75 percent of all pheasants fired at with the first barrel, and this figure should rise to 90 percent when a second barrel is required.

In order to achieve this commendable average, they bid us keep certain facts in mind. One is that pheasants usually either rise diagonally or else rocket straight up, and most misses result from shooting *behind* or *below* them.

A cock pheasant is about a yard long, and two feet of that yard is tail. Most of us unconsciously tend to aim at the center of the bird, and thus actually shoot behind or below it. Instead, try to imagine that the bird is tailless and aim at the white neck ring—which is an excellent target—and will cause the shot pattern actually to hit a vital area.

Once they are airborne, pheasants fly off at a speed of about thirty-five to forty miles an hour—somewhat slower than a green-wing teal, but still well out of the sea gull class. With a tail wind this speed is, of course, accelerated considerably.

A bird moving at 40 miles per hour travels eight or nine feet in the 0.158 second required for a shot charge (velocity: 900 feet per second) to cover 40 yards. The ability to judge lead comes with experience, but here's a good rule of thumb: lead a pheasant one length for near crossing shots (15–30 yards) and two lengths for birds farther away.

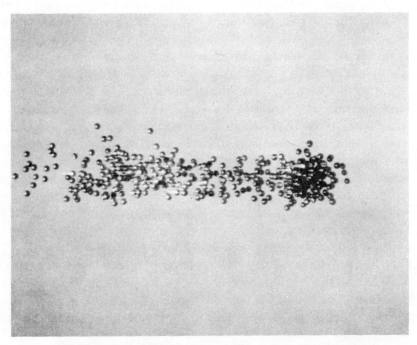

The actual shot string (full choked) leaving the barrel; not all the pellets will arrive in the target area at the same time.
Courtesy, Remington Arms Co.

It is also helpful in estimating lead to think of a shot string not as a flat disc advancing through the air (like the pattern it makes on a sheet of paper) but rather as a cone some three or four feet in length. If the first pellets reach the point of aim ahead of the target, later pellets will be passing through the area when the target gets there. Overleading is far better than underleading, and this conception of the shot string may make the hunter bold enough to add just a bit more to his estimated lead. Ask any duck hunter if he hasn't fired at the first duck in a string and seen the second bird fall.

TYPES OF SHOTS

There are basically three types of shots used in shooting at pheasants— snap shots, swing shots, and intercepting shots.

The first of these, the snap shot, actually affords the least chance for success. It's used much less frequently in pheasant hunting than in grouse or woodcock gunning when sometimes it is the only shot possible before the target disappears into dense cover. Once in a while, however, the pheasant hunter must use it, as when a bird flushes from a good distance and would be out of range if the hunter took time for a deliberately aimed shot.

Even under these circumstances, a snap shot doesn't imply firing from the hip, or pulling the trigger as soon as the stock touches the shoulder. Instead, these shots might better be called "aimed snaps" or, as the late Dr. Charles Norris, author of *Eastern Upland Gunning,* called them, "corrected snap" shots.

In executing the snap shot, the gun is raised quickly to the shoulder and fired—but not until a fraction of a second's pause has enabled the shooter to take aim or, in Norris's words, "correct his alignment." This hardly noticeable pause usually means the difference between a hit and a miss, and makes it different from the unaimed snap shot that many hunters use, even when there is no necessity for it. Novice gunners, especially, unnerved by a sudden flush and by the apparent speed with which their target is taking itself away, are prone to resort to snap shots when there is no need for them. This shot should be used only when there is no other alternative.

It is almost always better to wait and take an aimed shot at a bird since actually it isn't moving as fast as it appears to be. What form that aimed shot takes will depend upon conditions and also upon the man doing the shooting. Some hunters use both swing and intercepting shots as circumstances dictate; others prefer one or the other at all times. They are equally effective.

In a swing shot, as the name implies, the gun muzzle swings *past* the bird and the shot is fired when an adequate lead has been achieved. The swing begins while the gun is being raised to the shoulder and continues smoothly

The swing shot: begin the swing behind the bird, fire when your lead is right, and follow
through.

even after the trigger has been pulled. For there is a lag time between the time the brain flashes the message to fire to the finger, the finger responds, the hammer falls, and the shot charge leaves the barrel. This lag time has been computed for the average shooter. It might be interesting to give the figures here. Human reaction time between brain and trigger is .02 of a second, delay time between trigger and falling hammer is .011 of a second, ignition and barrel time .003 of a second, and shot flight time from muzzle to a target 60 feet away is .065 to .089 of a second—almost an entire second. In that .099 of a second a pheasant will travel from 20 to 40 feet, depending upon wind and whether it is a passing shot or a flushing shot. In any event, without lead, the shot charge would be far behind the target.

The intercepting shot: point the gun ahead of the bird; when you feel you have established the correct lead—fire.

In executing intercepting shots, instead of swinging the muzzle past the bird to the desired lead, take aim at a point ahead of the target. The trigger is pulled when the gunner's judgment tells him that shot charge and target will reach the point of aim at the same time. This is a fast shot, almost as fast as the aimed snap shot, and is highly effective, especially on straightaway or quartering shots on rising or dropping birds.

When a pheasant flushes from below and ahead, lead one length ahead and above and forget about that tail!

Occasionally, pheasants that flush wild or are flushed by another hunter may fly toward you and pass directly overhead. They are usually high and traveling fast, particularly if they have a tail wind, and under these circumstances they offer an extremely sporty target.

Expert shooters agree that these birds should be taken as soon as they come within range. The hunter's tendency is to wait for them to come close, but then if that shot misses, the bird will pass overhead and be behind the gunner before a second shot can be fired. That means whirling around off balance and often results in a second miss. Shooting the first barrel while the pheasant is well out gives the gunner time for a second shot while the target is still coming toward him.

This "incoming" shot is not particularly difficult (again I am quoting the experts) although it seems to give many gunners trouble. This is probably because upland hunters are so seldom faced with this particular shot. Waterfowl gunners, especially those who shoot in timbered areas, become very familiar with it and learn to handle it with little difficulty. Stoppers at the end of a cornfield drive have many opportunities to use this shot.

To execute it correctly, face the bird and raise your gun so that it swings vertically past the target. At the instant the muzzle blots out the bird, pull the trigger, still swinging. Hesitation or a pause in the swing will result in a miss by shooting behind the bird. If your gun has selective triggers, it's best to shoot the choked barrel first and save the cylinder barrel for the second shot, if needed. If the first shot misses, keep swinging and shoot again. A fast gun can get off two shots in four-fifths of a second, although the speed for the average man is nearly double that time.

A slightly different technique is required for high birds that pass directly overhead. If you aim the muzzle at their bills and then jerk the gun a few inches ahead, depending upon their altitude, they can be killed with encouraging consistency.

This is another duck hunter's shot, and it used to give me a great deal of trouble until a veteran waterfowl gunner showed me how to handle it. In a week of hunting in the Arkansas river bottoms, I never saw this man miss a single shot of this type. As the fast-flying mallards swooped overhead, he would raise his gun and mutter, "Duck, yo' daid!" And they were.

All of these shots—straightaway, crossing, angle—depend, of course, upon correct lead, and this is something every gunner has to learn from experience. It has to be personal experience, for no two gunners are alike in their reaction time, muscle response, control, and coordination. Even

The duck hunter's shot: on incoming targets pull the barrel past the approaching pheasant, even though the barrel momentarily obscures the target.

these vary from day to day in the individual. Fatigue, illness, anxiety, a hangover—all these affect one's shooting abilities.

We are all familiar with those days, regretfully all too rare, when we can do nothing wrong. Those are the days when we can't seem to miss even on the difficult shots. There are other days, and they seem to come more frequently, when we can do nothing right, when we miss pheasants that flush in the open at a thirty-foot range, and shoot a foot behind crossing birds.

The most common pheasant shot: a low-flying overhead bird. It seems like a dead-on shot, but actually you must shoot slightly under the target.

However, the better the gunner, the better his performance will be day in and day out, under average conditions of health and well-being. With experience comes the ability to estimate distances correctly and to know how much lead is required for a particular bird traveling at a particular speed in a particular direction. And I emphasize once more: it's better to overlead than underlead: don't be fooled by the length of tail feathers. Secondly, don't hurry the shots you take—ignore John Pheasant's feather-beating. If you approach your pheasant wing shooting with these two ideas in mind, your game bag is bound, over the seasons, to get heavier.

Pheasant Guns and Loads

Obviously, the most important item of a gunner's equipment is his gun. He may look like a walking model from Abercrombie & Fitch, own all the latest gadgets, game carriers, knives, and compasses, and hunt over a champion bird dog, but if he's shooting an inefficient and ill-fitting gun, there'll be more hamburger than game on his table.

SHOTGUN STYLES

Modern shotguns can be divided into five major classifications—single-barreled, double-barreled, bolt action, pump action, and autoloader. Single-shot, single-barreled shotguns have little to recommend them, aside from the fact that they are inexpensive and can be useful in teaching a youngster the fundamentals of gun handling and safety. With a single-shot a young shooter can learn something about shotgun pointing and recoil, lead and range. And he will learn to try to make each shot count, since a miss with his single-shot means that bird is gone forever.

Single-barrel repeating shotguns, of course, are another category. These include the popular pump-action guns, the autoloaders, and bolt actions.

The predecessors of today's pump-action shotguns were lever-action guns developed by the Winchester Arms Company during the golden hunting age of the 1880s. They were large, heavy 10- and 12-gauge firearms made for wholesale killing, similar to rifles of the same action. They went out of vogue with the introduction, also by Winchester, of the Model 1893 pump-action shotgun. It was followed in 1897 by the exposed-hammer model known as the "knuckle buster," the favorite scatter-gun of two generations of hunters.

When alloy steel came into general use in gun manufacture in the early part of this century, it enabled manufacturers to use lightweight parts which in turn permitted more advanced firearms design. The result in 1912 was Winchester's enclosed-hammer Model 12, perhaps the most popular pump-action shotgun ever developed. In more recent years the Model 12 has become a custom firearm and has been supplanted by the Model 1200 with its unique rotating bolt, similar to the one developed for center-fire rifles.

Autoloading shotguns are a more recent breed. The history of the earlier ones was marked with misfires, jammed shells, and other malfunctions

A single-shot Stevens shotgun. Courtesy, Stevens Arms Co.

A Remington pump-action shotgun, the Model 870 "Wingmaster."

Remington Model 1100 autoloading shotgun. Courtesy, Remington Arms Co.

which prevented the autoloaders' wide acceptance by the sporting public. The only autoloader that gained popular favor was the original model invented by John Browning in 1911. This gun was copied by other manufacturers, but as a class autoloaders did not sell widely during the early years of their existence.

Then World War II brought about a revolution in design principles and a functional improvement of semiautomatics for military weapons. With the return of peace, gun manufacturers adapted these principles to sporting arms.

Considerable research went into this work, much of it directed toward improving the appearance as well as the functioning of these guns. The original Browning and its imitations were distinguished by a sort of excrescence at the back of their box-shaped receivers. This was necessitated by the fact that the long recoil used in these early models required a barrel movement of almost three inches. In some other guns the breech block traveled backward for a distance greater than the length of the shell it was firing.

Then David M. Williams adapted the short-recoil system he had designed for military weapons in World War II to Winchester's Model 50 shotgun, thus writing a new chapter in the development of autoloading shotguns. The Model 50's autoloading cycle used a floating chamber as the recoiling member instead of the barrel and breech block as in former models. While recoiling only a fraction of an inch, the chamber thrusts a spring-loaded element down a tube inside the butt. As the element returns to place, it opens the action and the spent shell is ejected as a new one takes its place.

Remington Arms, under rights secured from Browning, came out with the Model 11, a long-recoil firearm, and later produced several variations of long- and short-recoil autoloaders, among them the famed Model 1100 that uses a gas-operated piston to complete the autoloading cycle. Some of the gas pressure built up by the exploding shell escapes through a port to activate a piston which works the breech block.

Winchester's Model 1400 is also gas operated and features the same rotating bolt head as the pump-action Model 1200. In earlier autoloaders it was necessary to adjust a spring to change from light to heavy loads, but the Model 1400's self-compensating gas system makes the adjustment for light or magnum shells automatically.

With these great improvements in design and functional reliability, autoloading shotguns have become extremely popular with gunners and are said to account for over 40 percent of all shotguns sold today.

The least popular of the repeating shotguns is the bolt action, pioneered by Mossberg and now produced by several other manufacturers. Their chief value lies in the fact that their usual three-shot box-type magazines give the hunter an extra shot over the doubles at a price in between the single-shot gun and the higher-priced pump-actions and autoloaders.

A Remington field model over-and-under with vent ribs, which help disperse barrel heat quickly. Courtesy, Remington Arms Co.

Mossberg's new bolt-action shotgun model 390K.

The Stevens Model 311 shows the classic lines of the double-barreled shotgun. Courtesy, Stevens Arms Co.

Double-barreled shotguns are still the favorites of a large number of hunters, especially upland gunners who seldom expect to have more than two shots at a flying target. Those two shots can be fired from a double-barreled gun just as quickly as from an autoloader.

Some of the popularity of double guns may stem from sentiment, for these were the traditional hunting firearms of generations of gunners during the great days of hunting in America. But more than that, I think, is the fact that no firearm exceeds the double in balance, maneuverability, and stream-lined beauty.

Names of the old-time double guns—Winchester, Ithaca, L. C. Smith, Fox, Parker, and the rest—conjure up mental pictures of upland and marsh in the bygone heyday of gunning. But some of these old-time names disappeared, others merged, and still others discontinued the manufacture of the classic side-by-side doubles. Happily, however, side-by-side doubles are making a comeback today. Winchester still makes the venerable classic Model 21, though now as a custom-built firearm retailing for several thousand dollars, depending on the grade. Ithaca is again turning out doubles. So are Mauser, Savage, Browning, and Marlin (including its Marlin L. C. Smith double). And good double guns can be purchased from Beretta, Bernadelli, Franchi, and Galef, among the foreign makers.

All these manufacturers and others as well also turn out over-and-under shotguns which have become increasingly popular in recent years. These guns appeal to shooters who like the double-barreled principle but prefer to point over a single sighting plane.

The better grades of over-and-under guns, like the side-by-side doubles, come with selective triggers and automatic ejectors, depending on the price. Not quite as balanced and streamlined as the side-by-side, the over-and-under still provides a very handsome and efficient firearm for the gunner who takes pride in owning a fine sporting arm.

For beauty, balance, durability—and expense—English double guns, both side-by-sides and over-and-unders, are probably unsurpassed; Purdey, Holland and Holland, Westley Richards, Boss, and Woodward are names known and revered wherever gunners gather.

In England, shooting sports are confined to the wealthy, who can afford to pay high prices for their guns. Consequently, the British manufacturer has a much smaller market, even taking foreign sales into consideration, than does the American manufacturer. The English gunmaker can't afford semiautomatic machinery, and since he must depend upon skilled craftsmen, he must also cater to the luxury trade.

In England each gun is custom built and fitted to the purchaser. A "try" gun, a dummy fitted with a number of screw adjustments, is used to fit stock, comb, pitch, and other measurements to the customer's individual requirements. The customer can also specify barrel length, weight, and other details he wishes to have incorporated into his purchase. And then follows beautiful hand engraving.

All this takes time and costs money. Add to that the import duty, excise tax, and dealer's profit, and it is small wonder that English guns often cost as much as a fine automobile. For those who can afford them they are worth the price. Those who can't can buy an American-made gun that is safe, reliable, rugged, and one that with reasonable care will last a lifetime or longer.

BARRELS

Having selected from among the wide choice of side-by-side, over-and-under, bolt action, pump action, and autoloading shotguns the gun best suited to one's requirements, the next thing to think about is barrel length. Long barrels have always been popular with waterfowl gunners, as the longer sighting plane makes for greater accuracy, especially on long shots.

In the old charcoal-burning days, long barrels also shot farther and with greater accuracy than short barrels. But with modern progressive burning powders, this is no longer the case. And for the upland gunner the advantages of a longer sighting plane are outweighed by the disadvantages of carrying additional weight on a day's hunt and swinging the additional length in brushy covers. For the pheasant gun twenty-eight-inch barrels are about right.

Since some Damascus-barreled doubles are still around and some unwary gunner might be tempted to try one out, perhaps a word of caution is in order.

Both foreign and American guns of older vintages usually came equipped with Damascus barrels. They were made by braiding strips of steel and iron into a band which was welded around a mandrel. The strips were joined into a solid piece by light hammering and the core was removed by drilling. Designs known as Laminette, Rose, Horseshoe and others were produced, depending on the manner in which the strips were braided together, and the results were often beautiful.

Damascus, or twist, barrels were adequate for old-fashioned black-powder shells, but they were not constructed to withstand the pressure built up by modern powders, as many a gunner has discovered to his sorrow. Burst barrels and injuries have often been the result of the combination of Damascus barrels and smokeless powder. These handsome old guns should be hung on the wall and never used afield with modern powders.

GAUGE

Gauge is another important consideration in the selection of a suitable shotgun. One can get into many an argument over the subject of the "best" gauge for a given type of shooting; here are a few random thoughts which may serve to guide the prospective buyer.

Gauge, as almost every gunner knows, originally was determined by the number of balls formed by dividing a pound of lead into equal balls. That is, if you divided a pound of lead into twenty equal balls, the diameter of each ball would represent twenty-gauge. Today, manufacturers have standardized diameters which closely follow these dimensions. The only diversion from this pattern is the .410 bore.

Most shotguns today come in 12, 16, 20, 28, and .410 gauges. Of all these the 12-gauge is the most popular among all classes of gunners and is probably the wisest choice for the average hunter who wants a gun he can use for various types of wildfowl and upland gunning.

One distinct advantage of the 12 is that if you run low on ammunition during a trip, you can almost always find shells in any crossroads general store across the land, but 16- and 20-gauge ammunition is harder to come by and 28-gauge shells are practically impossible to find.

The one disadvantage of the 12-gauge (but it is not an important one) is the fact that it weighs perhaps a pound and a half more than the 20, a difference which can be noticeable on a long day's hunt. However, for most gunners this disadvantage is outweighed by the greater number of birds it brings to the table.

Sixteen-gauge shotguns used to be extremely popular, and still have their proponents today. But they have lost out in popularity to the 20 in recent years among those who prefer a lighter gun. This is probably because of recent improvements in the shooting qualities of 20-gauge guns and ammunition.

In fact, there has been an increasing trend toward lighter firearms in recent times. Twenty and even 28-gauge guns have become the favorites of many hunters who speak enthusiastically of their light weight, easy handling, and excellent shooting propensities. And they're right, as a look at their skeet scores might attest. Still, these guns are only as good as the man behind them, and even then, in the final analysis they just don't shoot pheasants as well as the larger gauges.

If a person were to confine his shooting to woodcock, quail, and grouse, and if he were a better than average shot, he should get along fine with a 20- or 28-gauge gun. Pheasants, however, are large, tough birds. Unless they are hit in the head or neck, they can carry away a lot of lead. To my mind, therefore, the serious pheasant gunner should stick to 12- or 16-gauge guns. The .410 certainly has no place in any pheasant hunter's armament.

BORE

How should your gun be bored? There is room for argument here, but most hunters agree that all proper upland guns should be bored to have an improved cylinder and a modified choke. Everyone agrees, that is, so far as grouse, quail, and woodcock are concerned. When the discussion turns to pheasants, though, some experts and some gun manufacturers decree the modified and full-choked gun to be the ideal one for ringnecks. Nevertheless, I am going to refute their opinion partly because I am not as good a shot as the experts, and partly because I have the feeling that the majority of hunters aren't either.

Most pheasants, kicked up by hunters or flushed by gunners using dogs, give one a first shot at ranges of from twenty to thirty yards, well within the capabilities of an improved cylinder barrel.

If that shot misses, the target is still well within the range of a modified-choke barrel. A modified charge will bring a pheasant down at fifty yards (although the pattern gets a little thin that far out) if it hits a vital spot. Instead, all too often, shots at this distance result in misses or, worse, crippling. And most of us weekend hunters shouldn't fire at birds beyond this range anyway.

Even the old market gunners seldom used full-choke guns, though they usually said they did. Tests made on some of their old smoothbores showed these guns to have been bored "modified" in both barrels.

Therefore, in my judgment the average hunter's pheasant gun should be bored improved cylinder and modified, the same as any other upland gun. I concede, however, that if you're an expert shot and you do a lot of pheasant hunting in midwestern or western grainfields, you may bag an extra bird or two with a modified and full-choked gun. For the rest of us, east or west, it is better to use a wider-bored gun and pass up that occasional long shot in the interests of sportsmanship and conservation.

CHOKE

Choke is the constriction at the distal end of the barrel. Both W. W. Greener, the English gunsmith, and Kemble, the American one, laid claim to the invention of choke, but in 1875 a prize for developing it went to a man named Pape who lived in Newcastle, England, there being no other claimants for the honor at the time.

Whoever invented it, choke proved to be a very big forward step in shotgun development. Up to then, shotgun barrels had been true cylinders which allowed the shot to scatter widely soon after leaving the muzzle. By constricting the barrel near the muzzle, the effect was to force the shot through a sort of funnel, thereby compressing the charge.

Only the last two inches or so of the muzzle end of the barrel are choked, by various methods, some of them trade secrets. The amount of choke determines the size, regularity, and density of the pattern.

For example, a true cylinder barrel will place about 40 percent of the shot charge in a thirty-inch circle at forty yards. An improved cylinder will

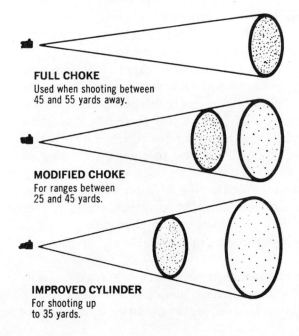

FULL CHOKE
Used when shooting between
45 and 55 yards away.

MODIFIED CHOKE
For ranges between
25 and 45 yards.

IMPROVED CYLINDER
For shooting up
to 35 yards.

The spread effect of the three most common types of choke. Remember that the real shot string is three-dimensional. Courtesy, Remington Arms Co.

place about 50 percent in the circle, a modified choke about 60 percent, and a full-choked barrel 70 to 80 percent.

Under ordinary circumstances, shots at pheasants are taken at from twenty-five to forty yards or less. Often they are outgoing shots. If the first barrel misses, the bird will have traveled only a dozen feet before a second shot can be fired. At that range a modified second barrel is adequate.

For single-barreled guns, pump actions, bolt actions, and autoloaders, the various choke devices made to fit the gun muzzle give the gunner a wide choice of choke—from cylinder to full. The only trouble is that, having set the choke at improved cylinder, your second and third shots, if needed, will also be fired on an improved cylinder setting while your target has moved into modified or full-choke range. Or, again, a bird may flush wild beyond thirty-five yards, leaving the gunner an impractically long shot for an improved cylinder. This situation can be remedied somewhat by loading a standard shell in the chamber plus two high-power shells with three-quarters of a dram more powder and one-eighth ounce more shot in the magazine. If you miss with the first shot, your second or third should bring down the bird.

THE STOCK

The stock of the upland gun is more important than in any other type of firearm. Shotgun stocks have evolved slowly through the years, from a crude block of wood (which the shooter pressed against his chest rather than his shoulder) up to the streamlined, padded stocks in use today. Basically, the stock should bind action and barrel together in a safe and efficient manner, and aid the shooter in aiming or pointing his gun at the target.

From earliest times, wood has been the favorite material for stocks and fore-ends, and remains so today. There has been some experimentation with plastic, and a few guns have even been produced with plastic stocks. But so far, sportsmen have shown a distinct preference for the older material. It may not be so in the future. Nylon stocks and fore-ends, like those supplied on Remington's Nylon 66 automatic-rimfire rifle, seem to have a lot of merit. They are light, durable, and resistant to chipping, peeling, or cracking.

The stock is particularly important for the upland gunner because shooting in brushy covers is far different from shooting on open marshes or even from a blind. For cover shooting you want a gun that points itself, a characteristic that only a well-fitting stock can assure. Poorly fitted stocks also add to recoil.

Too many gunners try, with varying degrees of success, to accommodate themselves to poor-fitting stocks. Experienced gunners know the value of proper fit in a stock and go to considerable lengths to obtain it, rather than being satisfied with the stock that happens to come with their gun. English custom gunmakers insist that the purchaser of one of their guns have its stock fitted to his individual measurements taken with the "try" gun mentioned earlier.

A correctly fitted stock can't make a mediocre gunner into a crack shot —but it can help. If the gun is right for the individual, it should be on or slightly above the target when it is raised to the shoulder, and should require almost no correction of aim.

DROP

Gun stocks are set into the receivers at an angle so that the butt of the stock is lower than the top of the barrel. This difference is called the gun's "drop." When a gun has a large degree of drop the stock is termed "crooked." When the amount of drop is slight, the stock is said to be "straight." Stock drop is measured at both the comb and the heel. To find the drop of any particular gun, lay it trigger up on a level table, then measure from the table to the front end of the comb and to the heel of the stock.

Normal stock drop for the average man is one and a half inches at the comb and two and a half inches at the heel. These are the specifications used often in factory-made guns. If the drop is in excess of these measurements, the stock will be too crooked for most gunners; if less, the stock is apt to be too straight. Too straight a stock leads to overshooting the target; too crooked a stock to undershooting.

It is impossible to detail in writing how to choose a stock to fit every individual gunner. Neither can most sporting goods store clerks tell him which stock is right for him. But here are a few hints to remember; then it is up to the individual hunter to choose his stock by trial and error.

A man with long arms needs a long stock, a short-armed man a shorter stock. Shooters with long necks require more drop than short-necked shooters. The shape and angle of the butt should comfortably fit the shoulder.

PITCH

Another important factor in fit is the degree of pitch at the muzzle. You can determine the amount of pitch by standing the gun up against a wall with the breech touching it and the toe and heel of the stock resting on the floor. Too much pitch tends to make the gunner shoot low; too little, to overshoot his target. For a gun with the average measurements of a 1½-inch drop at the comb and a 2½-inch drop at the heel, 3 to 3¼ inches of pitch is optimum.

Stock length is measured from the trigger back to the center of the butt, using the forward trigger in a double-barreled gun. Fourteen to fourteen and one-half inches is the correct stock length for the average man. A rough way to test for proper stock length is to set the butt in the crook of your elbow and tighten your finger around the trigger. If you can do this easily, the stock fits you. However, the best way to determine fit, as mentioned earlier, is to bring the gun rapidly to your shoulder and see if it is pointing at your target. If it is, you have a stock that is right for you.

Most American guns come with pistol grips, although today a few models provide a straight grip—which is standard equipment on practically all English guns. In this country we are so used to the pistol grip (full, half, or quarter) that we seldom stop to consider whether or not it is necessarily the best grip. English gunners are quite sure it is not. They say it detracts from the streamlined beauty of a gun and that it also impedes one's hand from slipping back easily to pull the rear trigger of a side-by-side double. Finally, they claim that a pistol grip tends to keep the muzzle low, thereby causing undershooting. But we are so used to pistol grips in this country that we have apparently learned to compensate for them without thinking.

Savage-Fox Model B-SE

The shotgun measurements that affect how it will "fit"; drop, pitch, and stock length. All these factors must be coordinated with the shooter's measurements to allow an accurate, easy line of aim.

The so-called Monte Carlo stock with its full-rounded comb is considered by some shooters to be beneficial in holding the eye at its proper level. However, this type of stock is more commonly found on skeet and trap guns than on upland guns.

PHEASANT LOADS

Today's shot shells can be obtained in a wide range of loads for every type of game from deer to quail, as well as for skeet and trapshooting. From this somewhat bewildering array of powder charges, shot sizes, and weights, which are the best ones for the serious pheasant gunner to choose?

Number 6 shot is probably the best all-around size for pheasant shooting, with numbers 5 or 7 as alternative choices. The finer numbers 6 and 7 are adequate for early-season gunning on light-feathered fall birds, and 5s are perhaps better than 6s in shooting late-season, winter-feathered old cocks. Anything larger than number 5s handicaps the gunner since there are fewer pellets in the shot charge. Anything finer than 7 or 7½ shot is more likely to result in crippled and lost birds than in clean kills.

All these shells come in both field and long-range loads, the choice being a personal one. High and low "brass" refers to the height of the metal base cup. The word "medium" should be substituted for "high" today since truly high-brass shells have been discontinued. Medium-brass shells include those loaded with high velocity and magnum loads. Low brass is the usual standard field load. (High and low *base* applied to shot shells is something else. This refers to the height of the base wad built into the shot shell. This height varies depending on the powder charge and shot charge to be used in a given shell.)

If you choose long-range loads, especially if you use a lighter-gauge gun, bear in mind that heavy loads make for heavier recoil. And heavy recoil often causes flinching and is detrimental to good shooting.

Long-range 12-gauge upland loads usually come with 3¾ drams equivalent of powder and 1¼ ounces of shot. Drams equivalent, incidentally, is an outdated designation of powder loads. There are 256 drams in a pound, each dram being one-sixteenth of an ounce. In the old days, black-powder charges were measured in drams. Today's smokeless powders are more powerful, so smaller amounts are required to do the same job. Therefore, 3¾ drams equivalent means that the amount of smokeless powder in the shell produces the same velocity as 3¾ drams of black powder. So 12-gauge standard or upland field loads contain 3 to 3¼ drams *equivalent* of powder and 1¼ ounces of shot. Drams equivalent are no longer marked on boxes of shells produced by most manufacturers.

Sixteen-gauge long-range shells are loaded with 3¼ drams equivalent of powder and 1⅛ ounces of shot, whereas field loads contain 2½ drams equivalent of powder and 1⅛ ounces of shot. Twenty-gauge long-range loads average 2¾ drams equivalent of powder and 1 ounce of shot, field loads, 2¼ drams equivalent of powder and ⅞ ounce of shot. So it will be seen that the 12-gauge gun gives an extra margin of shot that can at times mean the difference between a hit and a miss.

If you don't mind recoil, long-range loads will give you an extra ten yards or so of range, which makes improved cylinder and modified choke even more practical for pheasant shooting.

Here is a table showing the number of pellets of different sizes in various load weights.

Pellet Size

Ounces	9	8	7½	6	5	4
1⅞					318	252
1⅝				366	276	219
1½				337	256	203
1¼	731	513	438	281	213	169
1⅛	658	460	394	253	191	152
1	585	410	350	225	170	135

Pheasant Dogs

It is entirely possible to hunt pheasants without a dog and to shoot a good number of birds in the process. And as a matter of fact, a dog can be more of a liability than an asset at times in a standing cornfield full of pheasants, for example. But day in and day out, the man with a dog will find more pheasants, shoot more pheasants, and bring home more pheasants. And he will experience a great deal more fun and excitement on his trips afield.

The dog doesn't need to be a field trial champion. For that matter, it doesn't even have to be of a recognized bird dog species. One of the best pheasant dogs I ever hunted over (or, more accurately behind) was a raffish-looking collie-German shepherd cross with a few other odds and ends mixed in.

His name was Dinty, somewhere in his haphazard lineage there must have been some hunting dog blood, for he had as keen a nose as any dog I have ever known.

I acquired him in my teen years and it was completely by chance that his entrance into the family circle coincided with the early days of my hunting career, for I'd had no thought of using him as a gun dog. He blossomed first as a squirrel dog, skillfully trailing his quarry through the hardwood ridges, and barking frenziedly when he treed. His expertise in this department resulted in a number of squirrel pies.

And then one day as we walked across a weedy field on our way to a stand of oaks, Dinty suddenly plunged into a briar tangle and flushed a startled cock pheasant from its center. Despite my surprise, I managed to pull back the hammer of my single-shot 12 and bring the bird down in a considerably damaged condition. He tried to run, with Dinty in hot pursuit. The race ended quickly and the pheasant was delivered to my hand. That was the first of several dozen ringnecks Dinty found for me over the next several years.

He proved to be almost as good on woodcock and rabbits, and one day I shot a fox on a bird hunt with him. But pheasants were his first love. No ringneck cock could outrun him, and few escaped his nose. It had to be clearly understood, however, that *he* was doing the hunting and that you were a sort of junior partner suffered to accompany him on his expeditions.

Once he scented pheasant, he took off at a rangy lope, and if you wanted a shot it was up to you to stay with him. I ran full tilt across countless covers behind Dinty and a running pheasant. I was younger at the time and could usually keep within gunshot range in the chase. Hunting with Dinty was not a contemplative sport—but it was a rewarding one.

For more conventional hunting, however, one of the traditional gun dog breeds is probably a better—or at least a more practical choice—than the rare Dintys of the dog world.

THE SPANIELS

Perhaps the best breed of all for serious pheasant gunning is the spaniel, especially the springer. Although these dogs perform well with various furred and feathered game, they might well be termed pheasant specialists.

Spaniels as a breed had their origin far back in history. They were once known as "Spanish dogs" and derived their name from the Roman word for Spain, Hispania.

Springer spaniels have always been popular in England where, as far back as the sixteenth century, they were used to flush game for greyhounds and falcons. For many years no attempt was made to maintain separate blood-

A springer spaniel retrieving a hen in a state where hens are allowed in the bag. Springers will hunt and retrieve all game birds and small game. Courtesy, Larry Mueller

One springer working overtime. Springers are enthusiastic hunters; though they don't point, they flush pheasants expertly, and they'll retrieve, even from cold water. Courtesy, Larry Mueller

lines between springer spaniels and the smaller cockers. But in the early 1800s the Boughey family of Shropshire began to breed a pure strain of springer spaniels. Many springers today carry the blood of the Boughey spaniels in their veins.

Springers were popular in this country, too, up until Civil War days. Old prints and lithographs of the day show top-hatted, leather-booted sportsmen shooting at snipe, grouse, and woodcock flushed to their guns by liver-and-white or black-and-white springers. As settlers thronged west after the war, however, the spaniels' popularity gave way to fast-moving pointers and setters, which were better adapted to range the wide plains in quest of prairie chickens, sage grouse, and quail. Only in the East did the springer hold its own, in the grouse covers and woodcock thickets.

In more recent times, springer spaniels have come into favor again. The resurgence of their popularity coincided with the appearance of ring-necked pheasants upon the American hunting scene. In the southern quail range, setters and pointers still outnumber springer spaniels by a wide margin, but in John Pheasant's bailiwick the springer holds the honored place.

Whereas pointers and setters find birds mostly through body scent, the springer trails his quarry largely by foot scent. That's a definite advantage in hunting a bird that runs more than it flies. And springers do not waste time pointing where the pheasant has been. They stay inexorably on the trail until the flushed bird takes wing.

Finally, the springer is somewhat easier than a pointing dog for the average man to train. About all he has to do is teach the dog to quarter his ground, stay within gunshot range, and stop promptly upon command. In the hands of a good trainer the finished springer can also be taught to drop to flush and shot, that is, crouch when the bird rises and the shot is fired. But he will still be a competent gun dog even if he never learns these refinements, whereas a pointer or setter that fails to point staunchly is worthless as a hunter.

Besides being highly efficient pheasant finders, springers have few peers in retrieving crippled or dead birds. In the southern quail fields, a springer often goes along with the hunting party as the retriever. And no dog is better at battering his way through bull briars and brambles.

Actually, springers more or less train themselves, through experience. Some years ago, I owned a springer spaniel who still rates near the top of my roster of gun dogs. He was two months old when I brought him home and, although I do not pretend to be an expert trainer, I was able to bring him along to a point where he performed to my complete satisfaction on pheasants, woodcock, ducks, and, to a lesser extent, grouse.

Ruff, as my springer was named, eventually taught himself to head off running pheasants. Having trailed a sprinting rooster for some distance, he would frequently leave the trail and race in a wide circle to put the pheasant between himself and the gun, and then come in to flush it.

I recall a time when he chased a wing-tipped bird and, having caught it, carried it to a nearby brook and held it under water with his big feet planted on it until I came up, as if to say, "Okay, Mac. You're not going to run anymore."

What has been said of springer spaniels applies to the smaller cockers, with some reservations. They are keen-nosed, enthusiastic hunters and have always been popular among English woodcock gunners (from which they take the name "cocker"). However, whereas the average springer weighs in the neighborhood of fifty pounds, cockers—even the English ones which are somewhat larger than the American—seldom tip the beam at more than thirty-five pounds. Those fifteen pounds can make quite a difference in heavy American covers. The cocker tires sooner and is apt to be somewhat less aggressive than his springer cousin. Still, cockers are entirely adequate pheasant dogs.

Still another spaniel, the Brittany, has gained popularity in recent years. This spaniel, of course, is the only one that points, rather than flushing its birds. Compared to the other spaniels, the setters and pointers, Brittany spaniels are johnny-come-latelys to the American hunting scene, although they have been used by European hunters for centuries.

Some authorities believe that the Brittany spaniel was developed from a red-and-white setter which was the progenitor of the modern Irish setter. The Irish invaders of Brittany are thought to have introduced setters into the country, and so crosses of those dogs with local dogs contributed to the lineage of present-day Brittanies.

Some Brittany spaniels are born without tails; other have the tails cropped to a standard four-inch length. These tailless spaniels originated in France as a result of the mating of two tailless Brits, one an orange-and-white male from England, the other a liver-and-white bitch belonging to a native gunner. One tailless puppy survived and grew up to become a famous gun dog, much in demand as a stud. The litters he sired invariably included tailless pups or pups with vestigial stumps.

The modern Brittany was further developed through outcrosses with Italian and French pointers. This not only improved the Brit's scenting abilities, but also established the modern colorations of liver and white, orange and white, and roan.

The Brit is an enthusiastic, hardworking hunter—biddable, possessed of a keen nose and, like the other spaniels, an excellent retriever. Moreover, he is of an optimum size for transporting in an automobile, he is affectionate, and he requires somewhat less handling than the wider-ranging setters and pointers.

At one time the Brittany was dubbed an "old man's dog," owing to his somewhat slower speed and closer range. In recent years, however, these

The pointer and the Brittany spaniel, dogs with contrasting styles that you can match to your own personal way of hunting. Pointers range widely, and individual pointers sometimes learn just how close they can crowd a pheasant without making him run or putting him in the air before a gunner arrives. The Brittany works more closely and slowly, and so doesn't cover as much territory. Britts are the only spaniels that point rather than flush.
Courtesy, Hanson Carroll

traits have been improved by selective breeding to the point where Brittany spaniels compete with other pointing breeds on fairly equal terms in field trials. Like all spaniels, though, the Brit tends to hunt closer to the gun than do pointers and setters. But his speed and range are also entirely adequate for pheasant hunting. And a Brit uses both foot scent and body scent in his hunting, which makes him ideal for running ringnecks.

Although they are aggressive in the field, Brittany spaniels are somewhat "softer" than pointers and setters and can easily be ruined by harsh treatment. A sharp word or a gentle shake are far more efficacious discipline for a Brit than electric collars and whips. Once they understand what is required of them, they are anxious to please.

My latest Brit, Robie, was slower to develop than my others, but once he hit his stride, he became the best of the three. His fruition came suddenly. At three he still had a tendency to crowd a running pheasant too closely and often to flush it by trying to get too near before pointing. Early that fall, I worked him on a lead on preserve chukars that had been rocked before planting. Since I knew where the birds were, I could hold him in and staunch his points.

Apparently he got the idea. On opening day of the pheasant season, he came to a rocklike point at the edge of a field of knee-deep grass. When I walked in, a cock pheasant clattered up and veered toward the barbed-wire fence enclosing the field. I cut him down as he sailed over the fence, and he fell into a plowed field beyond. I tried to send Robie to retrieve, but he stood his ground, still pointing, and refused to budge.

"Go on, stupid!" I told him. "I've already shot the bird."

And at my words, another cock cackled into the air a few feet away. I lost a favorite pipe during the ensuing excitement, but I gained a favorite gun dog. Now Robie knew what to do, and from then on, he did it.

THE SETTERS

Setters have been popular with American gunners from colonial times, long before the pointers arrived upon the scene to challenge them. And in Europe, setters, which are descended from the early spaniels, have served their masters in the field since the sport of hunting began.

A number of strains were originated in England—among them the Featherstone, Lovat, Northesk, and Seafield, to name but a few. Some of these strains were brought to America, along with Irish and Gordon setters, and here they mingled their blood to produce what were known as "native" setters. And from them in turn, local strains such as the Chesapeake area Gildersleeves, New Jersey's Morfords, and New York's Campbell setters were evolved. Out of this mélange of English importations and American matings has come the modern so-called English setter. They are still a favorite wherever bird hunters gather. Certainly they are the handsomest of the pointing breeds.

Setters range more widely than spaniels, usually at a somewhat faster pace, and so they cover more country in a given period of time. Hunting by means of body scent more than by foot scent, they are apt to find birds faster. But this hunting method becomes a disadvantage when a pheasant runs away from their point.

To my mind, setters are not as good trailers as the spaniels, nor are they quite as good at finding running cripples, but many hunters probably will not agree with that statement. Certainly, the large ranks of setter enthusiasts attest not only to their owners' love, but also to setters' great abilities afield.

In selecting a setter, look for aggressiveness, grace, and sturdiness, as well as a hunting background in the pedigree. Don't try to push a young setter; give it plenty of time to find itself and to develop naturally. You will have a better gun dog as a result. Setters love human companionship, and the more you can give them, the greater will be the rapport between you and your dog as a hunting team. Once a setter has learned the tricks of his trade, he is less likely to forget them than is a pointer, and he'll learn them more quickly.

There are those who believe that the Llewellin is a breed of native setter, but actually it is one of the English strains, better known in this country than are most of the others. It was developed by breeding a pure strain of setters around 1790. Some of these dogs came to America and immediately gained a great reputation. As time went on, so great was their vogue that close breeding began to affect their field performance, and they began to

An English setter strikes a classic pose; his beauty is equaled by his performance afield.
Courtesy, Frank Woolner

decline in favor. Today there are very few purebred Llewellin setters, although there is some Llewellin blood in the majority of present-day English setters.

The Gordon setter took its name from the Duke of Gordon, who originally bred these dogs in Scotland. Also known as the black and tan, these dogs enjoyed great popularity among American gunners in the late nineteenth and early twentieth centuries. Somewhat slower and more plodding than other strains, Gordon setters nonetheless proved to be unsurpassed meat dogs for market gunners. But their dark coats militated against their wider acceptance by sportsmen since they were harder to see in heavy covers.

A Gordon setter vacuuming the air for scent of Ol' John Ringneck. Photo by Fred Itzenplitz

More serious than that, however, was the fact that more and more Gordons were bred for show rather than for the field. As a result, these fine dogs have lost their former hunting abilities. They are fairly rare today, and of those that exist few ever have the opportunity to hunt, which is too bad, for these dogs deserve a better fate.

What has been said of the Gordon setter applies in large measure to the Irish setter as well. At one time the handsome red Irishman rated among the finest of bird dogs. And for a number of years Irish setters probably outnumbered all other varieties of the setter breed in American covers.

Originally, the Irish setter was known as the red and white setter, although the red coloration predominated. (These were the dogs the Irish invaders carried to Bretagne where they became ancestors of modern Brittany spaniels.)

This Irish setter is wrapped around and frozen in the exact position the pheasant scent caught him in—a thrilling sight on a hunt.

Imported to America in the nineteenth century, they were a favorite of sportsmen and market gunners alike. But then in the 1880s the aristocratic Llewellins took over their place. The great popularity of the Irish declined and, unfortunately, owing to the beauty of the red dogs, much of the finest breeding stock was then channeled toward bench-show standards rather than field performance. From the rugged work dogs they had formerly been, the Irishmen turned into temperamental, high-strung prima donnas. Their powerful bodies became more slender and streamlined, their wide skulls more narrow so that, as some gunners disparagingly remarked, "They've bred the brains out of them." Gone were the great days of Donegal's Alizon, Joe Jr., Erin and Morty Oge, field trial champions all.

Today, however, the pendulum is beginning to swing back to breeding for hunting qualities. Sparked by the Irish Setter Club of America, a group of dedicated sportsmen is trying to bring the red dogs back to the field, and they are succeeding. There are Irish setters on the field trial circuit today, some of which have done very well—well enough to prove that they still have a place in the American hunting scene.

More than other setters, except perhaps the Gordon, the Irishman is a one-man dog. He needs the companionship of his owner and will more than meet him halfway. Although he's not as flashy nor as wide ranging as the English setter, he still does a thorough, workmanlike job of hunting to the gun. His points are not as classy as the lofty-tailed English setter, but they are equally businesslike and staunch. He is somewhat harder to see in autumn covers than are dogs with white in their coat, but it's never a real problem. Actually, some Irish setters do have a white chest as a throwback to their red-and-white ancestors. Certainly there is a no handsomer gun dog in the field.

THE POINTERS

If there is any breed that can rival the setters in popularity and ability, it is, of course, the pointers.

Pointers were not imported to America until many years after setters had made a place for themselves on this side of the Atlantic. But after the opening of the West, pointers gained popularity as fast, wide-ranging dogs, ideal for hunting on the plains. The reputation they made there led to their adoption by sportsmen throughout the country. And for good reason: there is no more efficient bird-finding machine than a well-trained pointer.

Although they lack some of the sensitiveness and affectionate nature of the setter, pointers will be extremely loyal to their master. More force must often be used in their training, since pointers can be headstrong and obstinate. They take longer to develop than setters and are more apt to forget their lessons unless worked frequently during the off-season.

Their great speed allows them to cover ground fast, but in thick cover their tendency to range widely sometimes works to the pheasant gunner's disadvantage. As in the case of setters, they may become frustrated by a bird that runs out from under their classic points.

Since they have shorter coats, pointers can stand warm weather better than setters and are less apt to become matted with burrs. Neither do their feet ball up with ice in winter hunting.

A field champion German short-haired pointer, in form. Shorthairs will point and retrieve a variety of game. Courtesy, John Rabidou

Pointers were bred for speed and ranginess, a fact you should keep in mind if you want a close-working dog for hunting brushy covers. If I wanted a quail dog for southern hunting, I wouldn't have anything but a pointer. But for pheasant hunting in thick, weedy covers—and on pain of ostracism by all lovers of this breed—I have to say that the English pointer is not my first choice.

German short-haired pointers, as a class, are much closer ranging, though considerably slower than their British cousins. The hunter looking for a keen-nosed bird finder that works fairly close to the gun and at a moderate pace—and is at the same time a top-notch retriever from both land and water—could choose one of these businesslike dogs.

The shorthair traces its ancestry to the original Spanish pointers, but it also has acquired bloodhound and foxhound blood. The result is a rugged, powerful, somewhat plodding dog that uses both body and foot scent in its hunting, can trail well, and can withstand the roughest cover and weather.

But don't look for too much style and speed. The shorthair is first and last a gun dog, not a field trial runner. In fact, German shorthairs are seldom entered in open field trials, where they would be outclassed in style and speed by both setters and English pointers. When occasionally they are entered in shooting stakes, they often acquit themselves creditably, and they compete strongly among themselves in breed trials held extensively throughout the Midwest.

These dogs are fairly recent comers to the American sporting scene, but their popularity continues to grow. For one thing, unlike other pointing breeds, their hound blood and stoic Teutonic personality permit them to be used for a variety of upland game and wildfowl. They can even be used for furred game it is said, although this encourages bad habits in a bird dog.

Shorthairs are gentle but aggressive, and more obedient and patient than the English pointer. But they have just as keen a nose for finding birds and an even better one for trailing them.

A young springer spaniel shows characteristic enthusiasm in presenting this ringneck. Photo by author

Another German dog that has caused a considerable stir among sportsmen in recent years is the Weimaraner breed developed by the aristocratic hunting set in Weimar in Germany about a century and a half ago. The blue-blooded huntsmen of the court wanted to breed the closest thing possible to an all-around dog—one that would point, trail, and retrieve under all sorts of conditions and combine with these traits the affectionate and gentle qualities of a house dog. With Teutonic thoroughness they set about achieving their goal, and to all intents and purposes succeeded. The genetics involved in producing the Weimaraner were never publicly recorded, but it is believed that the red bloodhound called *schweisshunde* was a major contributor to the Weimaraner's bloodlines, along with various other crosses.

Once the breed was established, great pains were taken to protect it from wide ownership and exploitation. It is said that there were never more than fifteen hundred Weimaraners in Germany at any one time, mostly owned by high-born and wealthy sportsmen, and none was allowed to be sold out of the country. Breeders were required to adhere to strict regulations. In 1929 the first of these dogs were brought to America: others followed shortly afterward. In this country, very strict breeding rules were laid down by the Weimaraner Club of America.

Under these circumstances the "gray ghosts," as they are often called, never became widely distributed. At one time the club even investigated the credentials of would-be purchasers to see if they were worthy of owning one of these superdogs. Quite a few persons passed the test, and there was quite a flurry of excitement over the Weimaraners for a while. Perhaps snob appeal had something to do with it.

In any event, Weimaraner owners were lyrical about the accomplishments of their acquisitions. Besides being unsurpassed pointing, trailing, and retrieving dogs, they were alleged also to answer the telephone, do the chores, and mind the baby. No dog could survive such encomiums unscathed; in recent years their popularity—or at least the fad—has waned.

There is no gainsaying the fact that Weimaraners are fine hunting dogs, and their dispositions and loyalty make them excellent house dogs as well. I have hunted over several Weimaraners and rate them about as good as a good German short-haired pointer—which is very good indeed. But to me they lack the style and speed of the setter or pointer (although they are better trailers), and their large size makes them less easy to transport than a Brittany. Nonetheless, there is no doubt that they make excellent pheasant dogs.

THE RETRIEVERS

Many pheasant hunters, especially throughout the Midwest and West, have come to the conclusion that the larger retriever breeds, such as the golden and Labrador, best fit their bird dog needs. Certainly, in trailing running ringnecks through wide fields and swales, and for finding dead and crippled birds, these dogs have few peers.

Originally, these breeds served one purpose and one only—retrieving. It was their job to follow the gun or to sit in wildfowl blinds, to mark fallen game and bring it to the gunner. It is only in comparatively recent years, and mostly in this country, that they have been allowed to range ahead of the gun, to flush game, and then retrieve. They have proven to be quite adept in finding and flushing game, and one of their specialities is the ring-necked pheasant. Indeed, this bird has been instrumental in changing their role from mere retriever to all-around gun dog.

The goldens' history is especially interesting. In 1860 an Englishman, Sir Dudley Marjoribanks, visited a Brighton circus that featured a troupe of performing dogs known as Russian trackers.

These dogs so impressed Sir Dudley with their intelligence that at the close of the show he bought the entire troupe of eight dogs. He was an ardent sportsman and felt that dogs as powerful and keen as these should prove valuable in the hunting field.

He was right. The trackers had long been used as sheep dogs in their native Russia, where their rugged builds and thick coats enabled them to stand the rigorous winters. They were said to have been so efficient in guarding the flocks placed in their charge that the shepherds frequently went home for the winter. When they returned in the spring, they found the sheep just as they had left them, although one is constrained to wonder what the trackers lived on during this period.

Trackers were much larger than the present-day goldens, weighing sometimes over a hundred pounds. But Scottish game was not of a size or ferocity suited to these big dogs, and it became the consensus locally that they were clumsy in covers. Nevertheless, Sir Dudley bred them for ten years in the hope of popularizing the breed in the British Isles.

Finally, in 1870 he abandoned his efforts and introduced a bloodhound cross which reduced the size of the tracker, improved its already keen nose, and slightly darkened its coat. Today the typical golden retriever weighs from fifty-five to seventy pounds. Its rich, golden coat gives it a handsome appearance borne out by its clean, powerful lines. The golden is gentle but not a coward; intelligent, and easily trained. It is indeed the handsomest of all retrievers.

The first golden retrievers to come to America were brought by retired British army officers to British Columbia around the turn of the century. They immediately became favorites there and spread up and down the coast from California to Alaska. Today they are still a favorite dog of western hunters.

The Labrador is the most popular of all retrievers today, based upon registrations in recognized stud books, and its popularity is well deserved. These dogs originated in Newfoundland rather than Labrador, where they were said to be used to carry ropes from fishing vessels to shore.

Although Labrador retrievers have been widely used by sportsmen in Great Britain for well over a century, their popularity on this side of the Atlantic dates only as far back as the mid-1930s. Part of this rise in favor was doubtless occasioned, as in the case of the golden, by their adaptation to the sport of pheasant hunting, as well as waterfowling.

The Labrador is a big retriever, averaging sixty-five pounds. His short, dense coat is well adapted to stand rigorous weather and cold water. The Lab is usually black in color, although one sees solid yellow ones more and more frequently. The so-called "otter tail" is distinctive of the breed.

Labradors give the impression of being strong, rugged dogs, which is borne out by their performance. They are among the swiftest and most

The author leads into a field with a brace of beagles. Photo by author

agile of all retrievers. No weather is too rough for them. They also have a reserved disposition and come under the heading of one-man dogs.

Besides being hardy and impervious to cold, these short-coated dogs do not collect burrs, a distinct advantage in many types of pheasant cover. The black Labs are easier to see in cover than the yellow-coated dogs that tend to blend into the autumn landscape.

If I did my pheasant hunting mostly in the Midwest and West, I might very well be persuaded to acquire a golden or Labrador retriever to be my gun dog. In cornfield hunts, the chief job of a dog is still that of retrieving, and when Labs are called upon to range out and find birds, they can do it with verve and efficiency. However, in the smaller, more varied covers of the East, I recommend smaller, closer-working—more pottering, if you will —breeds such as the springer or Brittany spaniel.

Finally, there is the beagle. Although rabbits will always remain his specialty, he is not to be scorned as a pheasant dog. He will follow the trail of a running ringneck with grim determination and considerable success. Some beagles have a special note that is reserved for pheasants. Hunting ringnecks with a beagle can provide some of the best elements of a bird hunt and a rabbit chase.

The beagle is by all odds America's favorite hound. He is an enthusiastic and versatile hunter and, at the same time, a loyal and affectionate house dog and companion.

Beagles are tough little dogs. They require little conditioning and training, aside from giving them plenty of experience afield—the more the better. They are somewhat reserved by nature, but respond readily to kindness and companionship.

PICKING A PUP

Whatever breed you decide on, there are certain things to look for when you choose a puppy. Unfortunately, it is impossible to predict certainly how any individual pup will turn out, just as it is impossible to foretell with any accuracy what sort of adult a child will become. There are too many unknown factors involved and many latent traits which do not show in early stages of development.

Again, as with humans, some dogs are endowed with more intelligence than others; some are ambitious, some lazy; some are timid, some bold; some are headstrong, some tractable. All you can do is choose as judiciously as possible.

A pup's heredity is perhaps the most important factor in predicting its hunting potential. If its sire, dam, and grandparents were capable bird finders, chances are good that it will be, too. Observe the dog's relatives, if possible.

Look for a well-boned dog with a sturdy frame and good conformation. The pup's eyes should be clear, and its teeth clean and white. And look, too, for an aggressive pup, and one that is friendly, confident, and active. From there on it's up to you.

TRAINING YOUR BIRD DOG

Having chosen from among the various pointing, flushing, and retrieving breeds the dog that best fits your needs, the next thing to think about is what traits should be stressed and what training given to make your dog a better pheasant hunter. These specialties can be suggested to the trainer or, if you take on the job, you can work on them yourself.

Some gunners hesitate to attempt to train their dogs themselves. If you aspire to ownership of a field trial competitor, it's wise to turn him over to a professional. However, if you want a dog that can find and retrieve birds adequately, if not stylishly, and provide close companionship afield, it's far more satisfying to train the dog yourself.

There are few greater hunting rewards for the time spent than seeing a dog that you have brought along from puppyhood make his first staunch point, and then run in to retrieve his first dead bird. There are a number of good books on the subject of training gun dogs, and by following them the amateur trainer can turn out a creditable performer in most cases. And, furthermore, it will be a dog that has been trained to do the things *you* want it to do in the way *you* want them done.

Take, for example, the matter of staunchness to wing and shot, that is, remaining motionless at the bird's rise and the shot. You can get yourself an argument any time on this subject. The pro-staunch people will tell you that unsteadiness in this department makes for unsteadiness in other things as well. This could be so in the case of a field trial competitor, but for everyday gunning, I have never found it to be critical. And in pheasant hunting I want a dog that gets in fast at the shot. The sooner he gets to the fallen bird, the better chance he has of retrieving wing-tipped running birds. Most dogs break shot, that is, move to the bird, unless trained not to, and I prefer to let them follow their natural instincts under these circumstances.

One quality to stress is that of control. A dog that becomes excited and pushes a running bird too hard will invariably cause the pheasant to flush when it reaches sparse cover. A dog that responds instantly to the commands "Easy!," "Slow!," and "Whoa!" will put more pheasants in the bag. This is especially important for a young, inexperienced dog that hasn't yet learned the refinements of pheasant hunting. I do not mean that the dog should be constantly checked or overhandled, which is a common fault of

A supreme moment for any pheasant hunter: a pup trained by your own hand graduates.
Courtesy, Frank Woolner

the amateur trainer. Rather, commands should be reserved for crucial moments, and then they should be promptly obeyed.

SCENT

Very little is really known about scent. What little is known has been learned largely from observation of bird dogs in the field.

Scent is made up of tiny, invisible particles, a form of gas if you will, about whose properties we can only conjecture. If we could only see scent currents, we would know a great deal more about scent's properties and how it is disseminated.

Some persons believe that scent comes from the bird's feathers or skin, others that it emanates from the oil bag or vent. Certainly there is a definite odor to the entrails, which even our dull olfactory nerves can detect. It seems likely, however, that the entire bird gives off scent.

It also seems likely that different species of birds give off individual scents so that a dog knows whether he has winded a grouse, a woodcock, or a pheasant. Additional credence is given to this supposition by the well-known fact that some birds dogs refuse to handle woodcock. It seems logical that a pheasant, being a much bigger bird than a woodcock, would give off more scent, but it may be that a woodcock's scent is so much stronger that it actually gives off more scent than a pheasant. Some dogs point different bird species in different manners and even trail differently, and some beagles, like my friend's Tim, sound a different note when trailing pheasants.

Another interesting phenomenon is the difference in the performance of individual dogs under differing conditions. We have all been out on clear, cold days with frost whitening the stubble when it would seem that scenting conditions would be ideal, only to find that our dogs are confused. The same is true on damp, rainy days. I remember well a damp, chill morning with a drizzle in the air when all the scents of rotting vegetation, mud, and dampness were exaggerated in my nostrils. My companion and I thought our dogs would find the bird scent equally strong, but instead they seemed unable to straighten out the trails of running birds, or to point staunchly the birds they did find. Yet on other, wetter days Robie found and trailed birds without trouble.

Easier to understand are a dog's difficulties on windy days when the scent blows hither and yon. And yet on certain days such as this, dogs will turn in a good performance. Various theories have been advanced concerning these puzzling complexities, but none has been proved. Perhaps birds' scents vary under different conditions. Weather, health, and dampness of feathers may all be factors.

Essentially scent is tiny, invisible droplets of effluvium which probably cling about the bird and are carried off by air currents. Some float behind the bird; others are left by actual contact of feet with the ground or of bodies passing through grasses and brush. Scent is apparently very persistent, adhering for some time to whatever it touches before dissipating. Dogs will often investigate a spot thoroughly and then pass on as if satisfied that the bird has been long gone. Often, however, when body scent is faint, pointing dogs will thrust their noses to the ground to pick up foot scent, which apparently remains longer. Blood scent probably is quite different, which explains why dogs will often point crippled birds and then lunge in to grab them.

We do know for a fact that moving birds give off more scent than motionless ones. That is why nesting birds are harder for predators to find, since their scent tends to dissipate more rapidly. It may be that the bird's act of exercising increases the flow of scent. We know that when a bird is killed in flight and is air washed in its fall, it is often harder for a dog to find than one that flutters about on the ground after falling.

These are all interesting facts to contemplate, and it's too bad we know so little about scent. This is a fascinating field for further research. Meanwhile, we can only be grateful that man and nature have conspired so successfully through the generations to bring out and improve the scenting qualities that modern bird dogs inherited from their wild ancestors.

Clothes
and Equipment

Clothes don't make the hunter, but they can go a long way toward keeping him warm, comfortable, and dry, if need be. And, if he chooses wisely from among the wide variety of garments offered by manufacturers today, clothes can add materially to his performance afield.

Today's gunners seem to be more sartorially conscious than those of a generation ago; you see fewer scarecrow figures in the uplands nowadays. Still, it must be understood that there's a fine distinction between old attire and disreputable attire. A neat patch here, a slightly frayed sleeve there, and perhaps a bit of fading are honorable scars of long service and sentimental attachment.

But this is by no means the first generation of well-dressed hunters. Nathaniel Currier's lithograph *Woodcock Shooting*, which dates back to the 1840s, depicts two sportsmen, complete with dogs, in a bosky dell about to fire at a pair of rising woodcock.

The scene is accurately and artistically recorded, but it is the hunters' raiment that catches the eye. They might be twin brothers, for they are garbed in almost identical outfits. Both are wearing broad-brimmed straw hats with brown bands around the crown. Both sport dark bow ties and white shirts, and one displays a sort of bottle green vest under a long tan coat that reaches to his knees. The other gunner's coat is buttoned so one can't tell if he is affecting the same type of waistcoat. However, both men's trousers are of a spotless white, and one is wearing knee-length leather boots. This, gentlemen, is class.

Today's hunting clothes, by comparison, would appear to be somewhat more functional and considerably more harmonious with the hunter's natural surroundings. This has been the trend in the evolution of outdoor clothing through the years so that today gunners have a wide choice of hunting apparel.

HATS AND CAPS

Starting at the top, hunters can choose from among a varied assortment of hats and caps. If you prefer a hat you can find them in cotton, felt, wool, or Acrilan. In the early part of the upland season, felt or wool can be a bit warm, and a hat of lighter material is more comfortable.

One hat with a great deal to recommend it is a brown camouflage duck hunter's hat made of windproof silicone-treated cotton and nylon. A wide flap folds up against the crown in dry weather but can be lowered to cover the back of the neck when it rains. And a stiff three-inch-wide brim keeps the rain out of your face. But its camouflage color, which is fine in a duck blind, is less appropriate in pheasant cover.

Fluorescent orange top pieces, which show up vividly at a distance, are available in similar styles. Even pheasant gunners aren't completely safe from hunters who shoot first and look afterward. You can trust the companions you hunt with, but there's always the fellow over the ridge. Besides, a blaze orange hat helps members of a hunting group to keep tabs on one another. You can get a blaze orange hat in Acrilan duck with a green underbrim to cut down glare.

Many gunners like hats, and there is no doubt that their brims protect wearers from sun and rain better than a cap does. However, hats are not as warm in cold weather, and further, stubs and briars tend to snatch them off one's head at frequent intervals. For these reasons, to my mind a cap is a more practical head covering.

Actually, a baseball cap makes a pretty good top piece for gunning. But again I prefer a fluorescent orange cap: a light Acrilan one for early-season and a heavier leather one with snug tabs for cold-weather gunning.

SHIRTS

Try a cotton flannel or half-cotton, half-polyester shirt for early-season wear. Cotton–polyester shirts are especially good perspiration absorbers on warm days. The noon hours of early season can frequently be summer warm, and a heavy shirt becomes an abomination under such conditions. Cotton flannel ones keep you comfortable on cooler days.

As the days turn chill, change to chamois shirts. They insulate you from frost but are still light enough to keep you from perspiring unduly as you wade through swamp and brush. And the chamois-cloth shirt is an example of a garment that improves, like wine, with age. The more they are washed, the softer and more comfortable they become, and they last forever.

Against the onset of really cold weather, nothing can equal a wool or Viyella shirt for warmth and comfort. Viyella shirts (made of wool and cotton) are somewhat lighter than the all-wool shirts and are almost as warm, though I grant that probably no material, except down, is warmer than a 100 percent wool fabric.

Whatever shirt I wear, I like to leave it unbuttoned at the collar and wear an ascot tie to keep the cold from seeping down my neck. Ascots are most comfortable affairs. They prevent collar chafing, feel light and soft around your throat, and help to keep your upper chest warm. I recommend them highly.

COATS

A hunting coat is apt to be much too heavy for the first weeks of the upland season. A light vest or suspendered game bag and pockets is far better. A vest that is especially good for warm-weather hunting is the model made of tightly woven cotton poplin with a nylon net back. It features a rubberized, zippered game bag that can be converted into a waterproof drop seat when not carrying pheasants. The wide front pockets are equipped with shell loops. Another model, made of fluorescent orange Acrilan, offers similar features.

The skeleton suspendered game bags are even cooler and there is enough room for a couple of birds in the game pocket and for knife, matches, smokes, and a chocolate bar in the front pockets. However, most do not come equipped with shell loops, and shells in a pocket soon become coated with dirt, leaf dust, and tobacco crumbs. To overcome this problem, I wear a rubber shell carrier that fastens to my belt and can hold eight shells. With my usual percentage of misses, I often have to replenish the shell carrier, but this is easily accomplished when I return to the car.

For cold-weather gunning a regulation shooting coat brings warmth and comfort. One of the best that I know of is a part Dacron, part cotton jacket with both slash and patch pockets, a rubberized, zippered game bag, and corduroy collar and cuffs.

Shooting coats should be wind and rain resistant and sturdy enough to turn brush and briars. Canvas and duck coats will do the job but in order to carry out these functions the material must be heavy to the point of stiffness. So I prefer some of the newer cotton-mixed artificial fabrics for their lightness and softness.

Unique hunting overalls of two-ply duck with a zip-off rubberized game pouch and seat. Courtesy, Cabela's, Sidney, Nebraska

PANTS

These same artificial fabrics are used in the manufacture of hunting pants, and in my opinion they constitute a great improvement over the old-time canvas pants or blue jeans. They're much lighter than the former and are far more briar and brush resistant than the latter.

Most hunting pants today are faced with nylon, leather, or Naugahyde. The leather- or Naugahyde-faced pants are unsurpassed for turning brambles and brush, but they are as stiff and heavy and as uncomfortably warm as the older canvas pants. They are fine for cold weather and for really tough covers but, for average covers in average weather, nylon-faced pants are much more comfortable.

Some sort of facing is almost a necessity, not only as protection from brambles and snags but also from rain-soaked brush that can drench you in a matter of minutes. If your gunning pants don't come with facing, you can buy waterproof and briarproof leggings to slip on over them. They roll up to fit in your pocket, are wide enough to pull on over boots, and snap over your belt like hip boots. Many hunters swear by them.

Besides facings on pants legs, other admirable features of modern hunting pants are rubberized seats and leather-edged pockets.

For cold-weather hunting I like 100 percent wool heavy-duty "guides'" pants. They shed snow and sleet and are surprisingly resistant to briars

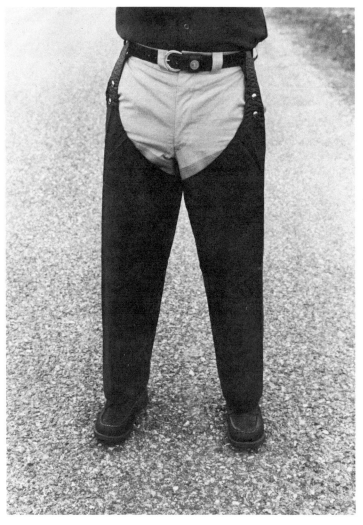

Leggings offer protection from early-morning dew and rain-soaked brush, and can easily be removed over boots and rolled up into a pocket. Courtesy, Orvis Co.

and snags. Their only drawback is the fact that they are almost too warm for active walking. And you can enjoy the same degree of comfort without the weight by wearing insulated underwear or longjohns under your regular gunning pants.

SOCKS AND UNDERWEAR

Most hunters like wool socks, but several gunners I know wear silk socks under their regular boot socks. They claim that the silk socks are absorbent, light in weight, and feel more comfortable next to their feet.

I prefer socks that are about 80 percent wool for warmth and the rest nylon for added toughness and wear. Some are made to stretch, so they don't bunch or sag after frequent washings. They provide the advantages of wearing silk under wool without having to put on two pairs of socks. To prevent chafing, the socks must be long enough to rise above the tops of your hunting boots.

The same people who like silk socks would probably go for the silk T-shirts and long-legged pants now available for gunners. Again, the idea is to have something absorbent, lightweight, and soft next to your skin, and then, except on very warm days, to wear some other type of underwear for insulation.

For early-season gunning, regular shorts and T-shirts are adequate. When the later-season weather turns chilly, I like some of the insulated underwears. One that is especially light is a Viyella set of pants and T-shirt of double-layer construction. The inner layer is cotton, the outer, wool. The inner layer absorbs perspiration, the outer shields one from the cold, and a dead air space between the two layers holds in body heat. The advantage of this two-piece set is that you can wear either top or bottom or both as required.

Another type of underwear that many outdoorsmen enjoy is Norwegian string underwear. It holds a layer of air next to the skin and keeps one warm at cold temperatures or cool on hot days.

For very cold winter hunting, nothing can beat a two-piece set of down underwear with stretch cuffs at wrists and ankles. The soft inner lining absorbs moisture and directs it into the down filling. The outer shell of nylon shields one from cold winds and resists water. It isn't often that you'll need underwear as warm as this, but when you do it's great to have it.

Some gunners still swear by the one-piece wool longjohns, and these too are satisfactory for most purposes, but I still like to be able to make my choice of tops, bottoms, or both, and think the new fabrics are somewhat lighter and warmer.

GLOVES

There is no question but that gloves protect one's hands from briars and brush scratches. And there is no gainsaying the fact that they keep one's hands warm in cold weather and prevent numb trigger fingers, an occupational hazard of the late-season hunter. Modern gunning gloves are treated to stay soft even after a number of wettings, a great advantage over the old-time gloves that become armor stiff under these circumstances.

For those who can shoot with gloves on, there are several choices, all of them adequate. One silk glove can be worn under light leather gloves. There are more conventional soft leather or pigskin gloves thin enough to make the feel of the trigger natural to the gunner and still be warm. You can buy fleece-lined gloves for cold weather, but their bulk can make it hard to find the trigger.

Gunners I know have tried several expedients to keep their hands warm and still stripped for action. One is cutting the index finger from the right- (or left-) hand glove, which only results in having one's other fingers warm while the all-important trigger finger freezes.

And there is the mitten with a slit in the palm, which theoretically enables you to wriggle your trigger finger out from under the covers when the occasion demands. I have missed a number of birds with this one. My expedient today is to wear a pair of cloth gloves and rip the right-hand one off with my teeth when it is time to shoot. This works better when shooting over a pointing dog than it does when a ringneck cock flushes unannounced thirty feet ahead, but at least it affords some protection for the hands.

FOOTWEAR

The most important item of a gunner's apparel is his boots. Nothing can ruin a day afield more than cold, wet, cramped, or blistered feet. The ideal boot should be light in weight, tough, comfortable, waterproof, and skid-proof. Fortunately, all these qualities can be found in a variety of modern boot styles.

L. L. Bean's ever-popular Maine hunting shoe, the favorite of a generation of northeastern hunters. Courtesy, L. L. Bean Co.

There are the rubber-bottomed pacs, the "swamp slippers" of generations of northeastern gunners, created by L. L. Bean of Freeport, Maine, many years ago. They are still as popular today as when they first appeared on the market. They are very light, waterproof for ordinary walking in wet, mucky areas, and, as the practical Mr. Bean advised, the rubber bottoms can be replaced when they wear out. They come in six-, eight-, and fourteen-inch heights. One's choice depends on personal preference and the type of terrain in which one hunts. I like the eight-inch ones best, as the higher leather tends to cramp the legs.

Russell Birdshooters are another popular boot. Their moccasin vamp is extremely light and comfortable for hard walking. Their tough knurled-rubber soles make them ideal for dry upland covers but not quite as practical for swamplands.

Many hunting boots today are insulated. But insulation adds bulk and weight, and the extra protection against cold it provides is not necessary for upland gunning. They can be an advantage when hunting late-season pheasants in snow.

Some hunters who do much of their gunning in swampy covers like slip-on rubber boots. These are certainly the most waterproof footgear one can obtain. They do tend to "draw" the feet, however, and bind the lower leg. They are not as comfortable for a long day of hunting as some of the other types of boots.

No matter which boot you choose, new boots should be well broken in before the hunting season starts, and leather ones should be treated with silicone now and then during the season.

ACCESSORIES

Some gunners like to wear shooting glasses. There is no denying that glasses help to protect the shooter's eyes from twigs, brush, and weeds, as well as to prevent glare.

Polarized glasses have another function as well. They transmit additional light by filtering out ultraviolet rays, thus improving vision at dawn and dusk and on dark days. They also help the wearer to distinguish objects more sharply in heavy cover, to see one's target better, and even sometimes to distinguish a bird on the ground.

You can buy several types of shooting glasses, but be sure to buy good ones. Yellow or tan are the best colors for lenses. Frames may be heavy-rimmed plastic or metal-rimmed, like the excellent Mitchell glasses. Some have a band or "snugger" that goes around one's head to hold the glasses on securely in brushy covers. Some can be optically ground to one's prescription.

Don't neglect the little items of equipment that can make your hunting comfortable—a drinking cup, a dry pair of socks, and the afternoon rest are hunting rewards in themselves. After all, hunting pheasants is fun, isn't it? Photo by author

HUNTING ACCESSORIES

Besides the clothing he wears, there are other items for the well-equipped gunner to carry afield. Some are essential, others are designed to add to the gunner's comfort or pleasure, and some are downright frivolous.

One essential item of equipment is a compass. Pheasant gunning is usually carried on in fairly open country, compared to the covers frequented by grouse and woodcock gunners or the big woods traversed by deer hunters. Still, pheasant gunners often find themselves in unfamiliar surroundings, sometimes under conditions that make it difficult to remain oriented.

I well remember spending a foggy morning attempting to find my way out of an extensive and extremely mucky swamp because I had forgotten to bring along a compass. I spent several hours slogging through ankle-deep mud with no visible landmarks to guide me. Several times I found myself in the center of the morass, and several other times I passed by a rotted, moss-grown log, having traveled in a circle. I was in no danger, but I was cold, wet, and tired when I finally came out into a field several miles from my car. A compass is such a small and inexpensive item that there is no excuse (as I tell myself now) for not carrying one at all times afield.

Almost any compass is adequate to keep your feet on the right path. Nor, for most purposes, do you need to take compass declinations or other scientific matters into account. About all you need to know is in what direction you need to travel to take you back to the road.

In order to do this, it is only necessary to know whether the road lies to the north, south, east, or west and in what direction you have been hunting. Then by taking compass bearings on certain landmarks—tall trees, mountain peaks, or rock formations—you can easily return the way you came.

The most common type of compass is the watch compass on which the dial is fixed and the needle swings on a pivot. Some of these compasses are fitted with snap covers. The advantage of the snap cover is that it not only protects the glass face from breakage but also prevents dust or moisture from accumulating inside the case, a condition which may affect the instrument's accuracy. Watch compasses are durable and serviceable, and there is little that can go wrong with their simple mechanisms. They are entirely adequate for the pheasant hunter.

Another type, the wrist compass, has a rotating dial floating in a liquid-filled case with just enough air space to form a bubble similar to that in a carpenter's spirit level. A luminous line bisects the movable face of the compass and two luminous dots indicate the sight line on the case.

Along with a compass, a government topographic map is a good and inexpensive investment, especially when hunting in unfamiliar areas. It will help you to use your compass in orienting yourself to your surroundings and, equally important, will enable you to pick out likely covers to explore. Since topographic maps clearly delineate roads, contours, swamps, pipe and power lines, streams, and other natural and man-made landscape features, they can give you clues to productive covers. With a little practice, you can get a very good idea of what the terrain looks like even before seeing it.

Another essential item is a good knife. It doesn't have to be large—in fact, shouldn't be—for bird hunting. Pheasant hunters' knives serve a variety of purposes, but self-defense is seldom one of them. Keenness rather than size is the important thing. A good jackknife is perfectly adequate. Other types of pocketknives come with one blade or a dozen or any number in between.

Gadget-loving hunters enjoy the twelve-bladed kind, an innocent and harmless conceit, though one wonders when the average gunner out for a

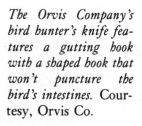

The Orvis Company's bird hunter's knife features a gutting hook with a shaped hook that won't puncture the bird's intestines. Courtesy, Orvis Co.

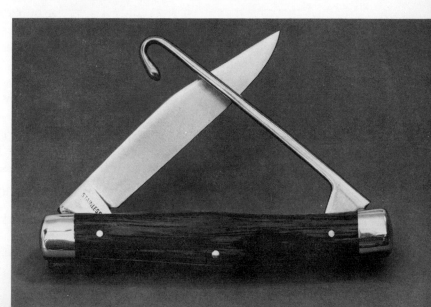

day's sport would require a saw blade, scissors, and a Phillips-head screwdriver. I suppose they might come in handy.

One gadget that *is* handy is the so-called "gutting hook" supplied with Orvis's bird hunter's knife. This is very convenient for dressing birds. It and a four-inch blade fold into a convenient pocketknife which fits unobtrusively into a shooting vest or jacket.

If you prefer a sheath knife, a four-inch blade will do all the things you'll need to do on a pheasant hunt. For upland hunting I prefer a pocketknife, which is less likely to become lost by being snatched out of its sheath by brambles or brush.

DOG ACCESSORIES

A whistle is a must for the man who hunts with a dog. Some gunners like the so-called "silent" dog whistle. I prefer those that give out an audible blast. Not only will the whistle call in the dog, but it will also help keep a party of hunters together, especially in heavy cover. Even if you don't have a dog, a whistle is a handy gadget to carry in your pocket.

A lead is a small but useful item. Of course, well-trained dogs that whoa and heel on command probably don't need a lead, but there are times when the amateur trainer will be glad to have a lead with him, especially when taking a young, eager dog into the covers or back to the car. I like the link chain leads with a leather wrist strap, as they fit into one's pocket more easily than do rawhide or leather leads.

A blaze orange collar has much to commend it. It shows up vividly in the thickest cover and is especially good on a dog that tends to blend into the autumn landscape.

Most pheasant dogs find plenty of water in the form of swamps and streams during their hunting, but sometimes in the warm early season when hunting grainfields, mowings, and orchards, it's a good idea to bring along a jug of water for the dog and a pan for it to drink from.

A thermos or canteen is certainly a must for humans who are less disposed than their canine companions to drink from swamps and streams. A jug of sweet cider is a most refreshing beverage in between covers.

A half-dozen assorted Band-Aids in one's pocket help take care of occasional cuts and scratches. And a chocolate bar or a small box of raisins help to reduce hunger pangs and provide quick energy when one is a long way from the car at midday.

These are the essential items—and ones that add pleasure and comfort to a trip afield. From here one can go on to various patented, folding, and completely useless gimmicks that still may be fun to own and that can serve as conversation pieces during the noontime lunch break.

8

Preparing
and Cooking
Pheasants

Wild game, as every hunter knows, can be delectable. Or it can be something less than palatable. The difference depends somewhat on the age of the particular bird or animal but mostly on how it is handled prior to cooking and how it is prepared for the table.

What constitutes good eating is a matter of opinion. Tastes change. In the days before adequate refrigeration, our forefathers' palates were attuned to putrefying meats which they disguised with spices and sauces and pronounced "gamey." Even today our British cousins are wont to hang game until it is, to put it euphemistically, high.

In this country, however, most of us like our meat fresh, or at least odorless, and few would follow the edict of earlier generations that pheasants should be hung by the tail until they fell. And yet many gunners today achieve almost the same degree of degeneration in their birds by the way they handle them or, rather, mishandle them.

CARING FOR GAME IN THE FIELD

When you compare the manner in which commercially processed poultry is cared for from packing plant to market counter with the nonchalant way in which game birds are treated between field and freezer, it is surprising that any of the latter reach the table in an edible condition.

Head-shot birds are off to the best start on their way to the table. More, unfortunately, are paunch shot, as deer hunters say, and in these birds blood and fecal contents of the intestines leak into the abdominal cavity and permeate the flesh. Perforated or torn crops, too, can cause a sour taste in the meat.

After the bird has fallen, it is usually stuffed into a game pocket which prevents air from circulating around it, and there it reposes, its cooling process retarded by the sun's warmth and the gunner's body heat. On good hunting days the dead bird lies crowded and matted by one or more of its fellows.

At the end of the day's hunt, the bird is unceremoniously dumped into the car trunk for the ride home. If the gunner is tired, as he usually is, it may be tossed onto a table in the garage or cellar to remain there until the mighty, but casual, hunter returns home from work the next day.

If one's friendly neighborhood poultryman left an unplucked, undressed, gut-torn chicken on a customer's doorstep during a warm October day, it would undoubtedly end up in the garbage can and the poultryman in bankruptcy. No matter what culinary miracles the cook performs in preparing that bird for the table, it isn't going to compare in succulence and flavor with one that has been properly cared for.

On warm, early-season days, pheasants should be drawn in the field. Some authorities feel that this causes the meat to dry out and that birds should not be drawn until they're ready to use, assuming they will be eaten within a reasonable time. That's certainly true in the case of birds shot in cold weather, but in warm weather I would rather risk having the meat dry out a bit than having its taste spoiled. You can replace the moisture in cooking, but you can't remove the spoiled taste. Even when pheasants are to be hung for more than four days in cool weather I prefer to draw them.

Looped-leather-thong game carriers, like the ones duck hunters often use, are really better than rubberized game pockets, for carrying game in the field. But if you don't care to wade through the covers with a cock pheasant bumping against your side it's still a good idea to remove your birds from the pocket while you rest or eat lunch or when you return to the car between exploring different covers.

Net hammocks slung in the back of a car or station wagon are better for transporting pheasants home than are closed trunks. So, for that matter, are back seats.

CARING FOR GAME AT HOME

When one arrives home, the day's bag of birds should be hung with space between each bird in a cool, dry place if they are not going to be plucked immediately. A screened porch is an excellent place to hang your birds. It is better to hang them from hooks, which permits air to circulate around them, than to hang them against a wall. There is some difference of opinion as to whether they should be hung by the head or the legs. I prefer to hang drawn birds by the neck to allow them to drain.

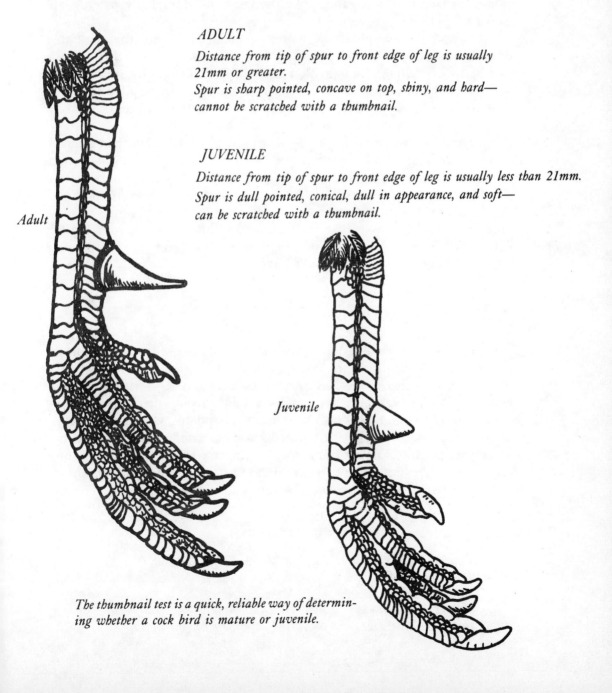

ADULT

Distance from tip of spur to front edge of leg is usually 21mm or greater.
Spur is sharp pointed, concave on top, shiny, and hard—cannot be scratched with a thumbnail.

JUVENILE

Distance from tip of spur to front edge of leg is usually less than 21mm. Spur is dull pointed, conical, dull in appearance, and soft—can be scratched with a thumbnail.

Adult

Juvenile

The thumbnail test is a quick, reliable way of determining whether a cock bird is mature or juvenile.

There is a difference of opinion, too, as to how long pheasants should be hung. The late Dr. Charles Norris decreed that pheasants should be hung for from ten to fourteen days. To my mind, or perhaps I should say to my taste, this is a bit long, but I do agree that pheasants are improved by hanging them for four or five days. Badly shot-up birds should be hung for a shorter time. No matter what length of time you hang birds they should not be plucked until they are ready to be cooked or frozen.

More than in the case of some other birds, young pheasants are better tasting than old ones. A cock pheasant that has been sprinting around the swales for two or three seasons, like the venerable domestic rooster, is apt to resist efforts to turn him into a tender dish.

Of course, it's completely a matter of chance whether the cock that flushes ahead of you is young or old. The chances are about three to one that he will be young, though. You can tell by examining his spurs, which will be knobs rather than the well-developed long sharp stilettos of old cocks. If you hold your bird by the lower bill and the bill breaks, the bird is young. Pinfeathers will also mark young birds.

Pheasants, like other birds, should always be plucked rather than skinned. It does take longer and requires more care, but the result is a much more juicy, flavorsome bird. Once drawn and plucked, the abdominal cavity should be wiped clean with a damp cloth—but under no circumstances should the bird be washed or soaked. This is akin to the practice of some misguided cooks who persist in washing fish and thus destroying their flavor. The only worse sin is parboiling birds to tenderize them, a practice guaranteed to ruin any wild bird's flavor.

PHEASANT RECIPES

If pheasants are handled with care and common sense from the moment they are killed until they are ready to be cooked, they have the potential to be a really delicious meal. But the finest bird can be sacrificed to poor cooking. Pheasants, especially, possess a subtle flavor that can easily be overcome by an injudicious use of herbs, spices, and oils, as well as by under- or overcooking. Conversely, in knowing hands, condiments and wines can accentuate the bird's flavor and achieve a culinary triumph. Here are some recipes worth trying. The first is one supplied by Ben East, a well-known outdoor writer, lecturer, sportsman—and gourmet. He calls it

PHEASANT AT ITS BEST

3 onions cut fine	1 cup chicken bouillon
Olive oil	3 slices bacon
1 bird, cut up	½ cup sherry
Salt and freshly ground	1 cup cream
pepper to taste	¼ cup fresh horseradish

Cook onions in olive oil until transparent. Brown pheasant pieces in oil, then salt and pepper them. Add bouillon, lay bacon over pieces, cook 30 minutes covered, preferably in an electric frying pan. Add sherry, cook 15 minutes longer. Add cream and horseradish and cook another 15 minutes until tender. The leavings in the pan provide the makings of an excellent gravy.

Ben adds another recipe, about which he says, "The greatest fish and game cook I have known is Frank Heidelbauer. The following is his favorite pheasant recipe. At the time he introduced me to it, he was an aircraft pilot and special enforcement officer for the Iowa Conservation Department. I rate this about equal to his channel catfish fried in butter, and I can pay it no greater compliment."

Split pheasant down the back and remove the keel of the breastbone, leaving the two halves of the breast together and intact. Stir in a half bottle of Heinz 57 sauce, ⅔ cup of whipping cream, and 1 tablespoon of liquid smoke. Keep this sauce hot and baste the bird every 5 minutes while it is broiling. Start it close to the heat and sear both sides, then finish at a greater distance from the heat.

Pete Barret, formerly outdoor editor of *True* magazine and veteran upland gunner, contributes this recipe.

PHEASANT IN SHERRY

Split the bird into halves. Put 2 tablespoons of butter into a hot frying pan that has a lid, and melt it. Flour the 2 pieces of pheasant and brown both sides in butter, then remove.

Now add enough flour to make a paste and add sherry a little at a time while stirring at low heat until mixture is the consistency of medium white sauce after coming to a boil. Add Worcestershire sauce to taste, a large dash of poultry seasoning, salt, and pepper.

Turn heat to very low, replace the bird in pan and cover, turning the meat occasionally. Cook at a bare simmer for 6½ hours, at which time the meat should fall from the bones.

Here is another which is a favorite of Bill Rooney, managing editor of *Outdoor Life* magazine.

PHEASANT IN WINE SAUCE

3 whole pheasant breasts, split	*½ tablespoon flour*
2 strips bacon	*1 cup white wine*
½ cup mushrooms	*2 tablespoons chopped parsley*
1 clove garlic, minced	*½ tablespoon poultry seasoning*
1 package dried onion soup mix	

In frying pan, brown pheasant breasts in bacon drippings; remove pieces.

Add to the drippings mushrooms, garlic, soup, flour, wine, seasonings, and blend. Then put pheasant breasts back into pan and simmer, covered, for 45 minutes to 1 hour. Serve over rice, prepared according to package.

Laura Heinold, wife of well-known outdoor author George Heinold, says this of her recipes, below: "I don't know how well you are acquainted with some of the views George has on game management, but I want to assure you they are very definite. For instance, he is always battling for less put-and-take bird stocking and the planting of more food patches to enable the birds to survive and thrive.

"Although hen pheasants are legal game in our state, George refuses to shoot one anywhere but on a game preserve. He contends the pheasant population is too slim to justify the shooting of hens. So what happens? Other wives get the nice tender hens to cook, while I always get some tough old rooster that George has chased from thicket to thicket. So I have had to take drastic measures in order to even make the bird chewable."

She has succeeded very well in these two recipes:

BRAISED PHEASANT

Cut older birds in pieces as you would a frying chicken. Coat with seasoned flour, brown in a small quantity of bacon fat in an iron frying pan, or spider, preferably. Transfer pieces to a casserole, add 1 cup of boiling water and 1 cup dry wine to the drippings in the frying pan, and stir well. Then pour it over the pheasant. Bake in a slow oven (275°) an hour or more until tender. Pour off liquid into saucepan and thicken it to make gravy. Pour this over the bird in the casserole and serve.

PHEASANT AND DUMPLINGS

Place cut-up pheasant in a large, heavy kettle or Dutch oven. Pour enough water over to cover. Add 2 cups diced carrots, 1 cup diced onion, 1 cup diced celery, and 1 cup finely shredded cabbage. Bring to a boil and turn heat to simmer slowly until nearly tender. Add 2 cups diced potatoes, 2 tablespoons butter, salt and pepper to taste. Cook until meat and vegetables are tender. Make dumplings to serve with the pheasant.

David Michael Duffy, eminent dog man and gunner who runs the Willow Creek Club in Wild Rose, Wisconsin, offers the following tasty recipe:

PHEASANT CASSEROLE

1 cup uncooked wild rice	*½ cup margarine or butter*
½ cup chopped onion	*¼ cup flour*

1 6-ounce can sliced mushrooms
chicken broth (or dissolved bouillon cubes)
1½ cups milk
2 cups diced pheasant
¼ cup pimiento

2 tablespoons parsley flakes
1½ teaspoons salt
¼ teaspoon pepper
½ cup slivered blanched almonds

Prepare rice according to package. Cook onion in butter until tender but not brown. Remove from heat; stir in flour. Drain mushrooms, reserving liquid. Add enough broth to liquid to make 1½ cups. Gradually stir into flour mixture, add milk, and cook, stirring constantly until thick. Add rice, mushrooms, pheasant, pimiento, parsley, salt, and pepper. Place in 2-quart casserole. Sprinkle with almonds. Bake in 350° oven for 25 to 30 minutes. Serves 6.

John Cartier, midwestern outdoor writer and gunner, says, "I'm great on charcoaling all game, even grouse, which are even drier than pheasants. The trick is to use very few charcoals under the grill so that the meat cooks slowly. I cut my birds in half. Then I place a sheet of foil over the grill and poke a lot of holes in it with a fork. The holes allow the charcoal flavor to get to the meat while the foil prevents the juices from dripping on the coals. Sometimes my wife will cook birds in a roaster till they're nearly done, and then I'll put them over charcoal for browning. When I start from scratch, I allow at least an hour for cooking. That sounds like a long time for birds cut in halves, but it's low heat that keeps them from drying out. Here's a roast pheasant recipe that we like to use:"

ROAST PHEASANT AND CRANBERRIES

1 pheasant, whole
1 teaspoon salt
¼ teaspoon ground pepper
1 bay leaf
½ garlic clove
1 clove
1 slice onion
1 slice lemon
2 tablespoons chopped celery leaves

1 tablespoon chopped parsley
2 slices bacon
6 small white onions
1 cup chicken broth
¼ cup Madeira
flour
1 cup cranberries
⅓ cup currant jelly
4 mushroom caps

Wipe the pheasant with a damp cloth and set giblets aside. Rub bird with 1 teaspoon salt and ¼ teaspoon pepper. Place bay leaf, garlic, clove, onion slice, chopped celery, and parsley inside the bird. Cover breast with bacon slices. Truss and place in roasting pan with giblets and onions around it. Pour chicken broth and Madeira over bird and sprinkle with salt. Cover and roast in a 350° oven for 1 hour. Remove the bacon and continue roasting for another 15 minutes. Thicken strained broth with flour, add cranberries and jelly. Add more Madeira if desired. Pour over bird and garnish with sautéed mushroom caps.

If you have time on your hands and want to be truly fancy, you can try this haute cuisine recipe from *la belle France*.

SALMIS DE FAISAN

Roast a pheasant until it is three-quarters cooked. Joint and skin the pieces. Put them in a buttered pan and cover with 1 cup mushrooms. Pour on ½ cup concentrated bouillon. Keep hot, not letting it come to a boil.

Chop the carcass and trimmings and brown them lightly in a pan in which have been cooked a mixture of 2 small carrots, ½ cup onions, ¼ cup celery, and 3½ ounces of raw ham. Add this plus 1 cup white wine to the chopped carcass and trimmings and cook for 15 minutes. Strain the sauce through a fine strainer, pressing with a spoon to extract all the juices from the meat and vegetables. Then strain again through muslin. Cook this sauce down. Add 2 tablespoons blazing brandy and 4 tablespoons butter. Heat, taking care not to allow the mixture to boil.

Drain the pheasant. Arrange the pieces in a shallow bowl. Pour the hot sauce over them and garnish with slices of bread fried in butter, and spread with a pâté made of the giblets.

A bit less complicated, but still extremely tasty, is this recipe which is popular in midwestern pheasant-hunting circles.

BARBECUED PHEASANT

3 pheasant breasts	*¼ teaspoon dry mustard*
1 onion, sliced	*½ teaspoon sugar*
paprika	*¾ tablespoon Worcestershire sauce*
2 bay leaves	*⅓ cup vinegar*
1 cup tomato juice	*dash Tabasco sauce*
1 teaspoon salt	*½ stick butter*
1 teaspoon pepper	

Put pheasant breasts, skin side up, in a shallow pan. Place slices of onion under each breast. Dust with paprika. Mix the remaining ingredients into a sauce and pour over the pheasant pieces. Bake at 300° for 1½ hours or until done, basting occasionally with the sauce.

Here is another good casserole recipe:

2 packages frozen broccoli spears	*1 small can mushroom buttons*
½ lemon	*1 cup sherry*
4 halved pheasant breasts	*1 cup sour cream*
1 can mushroom soup	*paprika*

Cook the broccoli and place in a flat, buttered pan. Squeeze lemon juice over the broccoli. Place pheasant breasts on the broccoli, skin side up. Combine soup, mushroom buttons, sherry, and cream and pour over the pheasant pieces. Sprinkle with paprika and bake at 350° for 1 hour. Serve with wild rice, prepared according to package.

From Mac Brown, who formerly ran the Macalong Pheasant Shooting Preserve in Philmont, New York, and who still busts plenty of birds, clay and feathered, each season comes this recipe supplied by his wife, Irene.

ROAST PHEASANT

Rub the inside and outside of a pheasant with butter and sprinkle with salt. Cover breast with salt pork or fat bacon, quite thin. Stuff bird with seedless grapes. If not available, use any solid variety of grapes. Sew together and truss. Roast uncovered in a very hot (450°) oven for 15 minutes. Baste at 5-minute intervals with pan drippings. When browned, reduce heat to moderate (350°). Cooking proceeds for 1 hour, basting every 15 minutes. Remove salt pork or bacon from breast of bird, and pour a wine glass of sherry into the roasting pan, together with a handful of grapes. Cook an additional 15 minutes. Total cooking time: 1½ hours. If the sherry cooks down too much, a little more should be added toward the end. For best results cook in a brown earthenware dish and serve in the same.

Here are some special complements for pheasant dinners:

HOT CURRANT JELLY SAUCE

Remove roasted pheasant from pan, skim excess fat from juices. Place pan drippings over low flame and add gradually a 12-ounce glass of red currant jelly. Stir until jelly has melted and then pour in 1 cup of good sherry or port wine and a heaping tablespoon of grated orange peel. Use only outer rind, with none of the white underlayer. Orange peel should preferably be dried out. Simmer gently while stirring for a few minutes. Serve very hot in a gravy boat. This sauce is an ultradelicious accompaniment to a delicious roast.

Another good complement for game is a bread sauce. Here is how to make one.

1 cup bread crumbs	*½ teaspoon salt*
2 cups milk	*¼ teaspoon ground pepper*
6 cloves	*¼ cup butter*
1 small onion chopped	*1 bay leaf (optional)*

Cook bread crumbs and milk with the cloves and onion, stirring occasionally until the sauce is thick. Remove cloves. Season with salt and pepper and add butter. For those who like the taste, a bay leaf may be added when cooking.

Lurton Blassingame, a distinguished authors' representative and a man with considerable skill in pointing a shotgun, offers this recipe which his wife, Peggie, created:

> "Cut rhubarb stalks in lengths of approximately an inch so they seem to be cubes. Place them in a pan, not touching one another, and freeze quickly. Then place them in bags and store them in the freezer. Since they are already frozen, they do not stick together and can be removed from the bags in any desired number any time of year.
>
> "When cooking whole birds, either grouse or pheasant, place about 8 rhubarb cubes inside the cavity. With a dry bird, such as a pheasant, add a little sausage and a piece of apple to the stuffing. Cover the breast with bacon strips while roasting, but remove them toward the end to allow the skin to brown. The rhubarb adds a piquant taste to the bird."

Every rule has its exception, and California outdoor writer Jim Martin provides this recipe in which birds are skinned rather than plucked. Here is how the Martin family cook pheasants:

> "One, don't pluck the bird ... skin it. Two, remove each side of the breast in a single piece. Three, cut each piece into thin slices. Four, make mixture of beaten eggs and cream. Dip each slice into the mixture, roll in unseasoned bread crumbs. Brown quickly on each side in a frying pan in which you have placed a slight amount of light cooking oil. Brown —don't deep fry—about 30 to 45 seconds per side. Serve with lemon wedges. You can also bone the legs and fix them the same way or stew the legs in wine.

Certain accompanying foods and beverages will enhance your pheasant dinner. Creamed or braised celery, wild rice, tomatoes, green beans, peas, mushrooms, corn, and tossed salads with oil-and-vinegar dressing are good choices, as are mashed, baked, or scalloped potatoes.

White wines are generally recommended with white-meat birds, though there is really no reason you can't substitute a red wine or a rosé if you prefer. Among the white wines, any of the drier varieties are always appropriate to complement a pheasant dinner.

9

Pheasants, Pen-Reared and Wild

More than any other game birds, pheasants lend themselves to artificial propagation and rearing. Game farm turkeys, for example, lack the hardiness to survive when liberated and are less fertile than their wild counterparts. Attempts to raise ruffed grouse on game farms have met with little success, and the woodcock's habits militate against any efforts to raise this species in captivity. Even pen-reared quail are apt to be weak-flying, frail birds, quite unlike the hardy, fast-flying bobwhites that result from natural propagation.

The pheasant alone can be hatched and reared under controlled artificial conditions and still be strong on the wing and exhibit some of the wildness and wariness of a native bird, if not its hardiness, when released. These characteristics, plus the fact that pheasants are the most sought-after upland game birds in America, make pheasant raising by both state conservation departments and shooting preserve operators big business with a capital B.

Pheasants are unique among game birds, as pen-raised birds like these will show all the characteristics of their wild counterparts when released into natural surroundings.

PHEASANT FARMS

A great deal has been learned about pheasant farming since the first pheasant-rearing experiments were conducted before the turn of the century. Today's game farms are operated with all the scientific know-how and elaborate equipment of commercial poultry enterprises.

The state game farm operated by the Massachusetts Division of Fisheries and Game at Wilbraham is a typical modern pheasant farm. Mating activity may begin with the increased crowing of cocks as early as late February. In the snow belt states, the true nesting season does not begin until April and lasts through June. This same timetable is reflected in the behavior of farm-reared pheasants. Just before and during the mating season, the birds at Wilbraham are given high-protein breeding pellets to help nature along.

By mid-April, mating is well under way, with the half dozen or so hens provided for each cock. The hens begin to lay eggs; some on the bare ground, some in rudely fashioned nests. At the Massachusetts facility these fertilized eggs are gathered and placed in batteries of incubators—seventeen thousand eggs a week from mid-April till late June. The incubation period is twenty-three to twenty-four days, and the average hatch is 76 percent, or about thirteen thousand chicks, about half cocks and half hens.

The day-old chicks are sexed. At Wilbraham this is accomplished by a method known as sex-linked down color, developed by Bernard Wentworth and J. Robert Smith of the University of Massachusetts, and E. Michael Pollack of the Massachusetts Department of Fisheries and Game.

In 1941, J. H. Bruckner, another game biologist, had discovered a "dilution effect"—a lightening of color tones of pheasant plumage—which was inherited as a "unifactoral sex-linked recessive." That is, a lesser hereditary trait, in this case lighter plumage, that is usually not apparent (since it is covered by the dominant trait) was made visible in one sex only. He found cocks less affected than hens, and noticed that sufficient dilution took place to distinguish the sexes even in the presence of the dominant melanistic (black) gene.

The Massachusetts researchers, after visits to several northeastern pheasant breeders, secured six cocks from a flock exhibiting the characteristics described by Bruckner. Each of these potentially "dilute" cocks was mated with eight to fifteen Chinese pheasant hens of unknown bloodlines. These were called wild-type hens. The eggs were marked to identify the sires and were then hatched at Wilbraham. The down colors of the chicks were noted, after which the chicks were autopsied and sexed.

The six cocks mated to wild-type hens all sired chicks that could be sexed on the basis of down color. The progeny of three of the six cocks differed genetically, however, from the progeny of the other three. The first group produced two down variations. The cocks exhibited the wild-type hens' down color, and the females were uniformly blond. The second group produced four down variations, which were listed as wild-type, chocolate, blond, and tan. The wild-type and chocolate chicks all proved to be males, the blond and tan all females.

This is only a superficial treatment of a highly complex subject, but the results of the researchers' experiments with further matings proved that chicks can be sexed by their down color and markings. Thus it is now possible to process thousands of chicks in a short time without handling them, and with much more accurate results than those obtained by using the older sexing methods. Most of the female chicks are sold to other states.

Day-old game farm chicks. Pheasants are highly manageable and can easily be raised by sportsmen's groups and other interested parties. Courtesy, Massachusetts Division of Fisheries and Game

From the incubators the sexed chicks, mostly cocks, are removed to brooder houses where they spend the next eight weeks. Here they are fed starter mash, but later, growing mash on the ranges to which they are removed at the end of the eight weeks.

Mortality from all causes runs from 8 to 10 percent. Various diseases attack both chicks and adult birds, and in former times raised mortality rates considerably. Today, advances in medical science and the discovery of new miracle drugs have given hatchery men potent weapons with which to combat pheasant diseases.

Coccidiosis and gapes (caused by a parasitic throat worm) used to be deadly killers of pheasant chicks, but today sulfaquinoxaline added to starter mash controls coccidiosis, and Tramisol destroys the worm which causes gapes.

Both eastern and western equine encephalitis remain a threat to wild and pen-reared pheasants—and also, for that matter, to man. (The word "encephalitis" means inflammation of the brain, the term equine is used because the disease was first discovered in horses.) Its cause, a virus, was not definitely established until 1930, when it was isolated by a group of scientists studying an outbreak of encephalitis among horses in southern California. Up until this time, deaths from this disease had been attributed to botulism and other forms of poisoning. In 1933 an epidemic broke out along the east coast and was shown to be due to a virus distinct from the western strain. The eastern type is much more severe than the western.

The disease is transmitted by the bite of a mosquito. Thus, the most dangerous and fertile areas for the spread of encephalitis among wild birds are large swamps inhabited by both mosquitoes and pheasants. Virus-bearing mosquitoes bite the pheasants, which in turn infect virus free mosquitoes, and eventually mosquitoes infected by biting the birds transmit the disease to horses and man.

Among pen-reared pheasants, the infection spreads rapidly by the birds pecking one another. If healthy birds peck an infected bird and draw blood, they will themselves become infected. In an effort to prevent pecking, hatchery birds are fitted with blinders or "peepers" which discourage this habit.

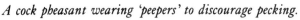

A cock pheasant wearing 'peepers' to discourage pecking.

The major effort to control the disease, of course, consists in spraying hatchery buildings and ranges and also mosquito-infested habitats of wild birds. Despite these measures, however, epidemics of equine encephalitis sometimes break out. Only recently, the entire pheasant population of a game farm in New Hampshire was destroyed owing to an outbreak of this disease.

Scrupulous cleanliness is the byword in rearing pheasants. Incubators, brooder houses, and ranges must be disinfected between hatchings, and the buildings must be kept spotless the year round.

Some of the young pheasants are stocked at seventeen weeks; the rest, hatched later in the spring, are released in October and periodically during the hunting season through November.

RAISING PHEASANTS

Besides the large operations carried on by state game departments and public shooting-preserve owners, a number of pheasants are reared each year by individuals and by sportsmen's clubs. The number of birds raised this way may range from one or two dozen to a hundred or more, but the sum total of these ventures adds many thousands of pheasants to the supply available for the fall harvest.

Some states will supply fertile eggs, up to a certain number, to residents upon the condition that at least half of the birds raised to stocking size be released on lands open to public hunting. For the farmer or gunner, raising a few pheasants can be an enjoyable and rewarding experience.

Farmers who raise chickens can start from scratch by incubating fertile eggs under a setting hen. It has been found that the eggs do not ship well and are apt to show a poor hatching ratio. If possible, it is best to pick up the eggs personally from a game farm or other source. They should be stored on a rack or tray for at least forty-eight hours in a cool, dark spot with the small ends down; the rack should be turned daily. For best results, the eggs should be set before they are ten days old.

A medium-sized hen can brood twenty-five or thirty pheasants but can incubate only about eighteen. Sometimes two hens can be set with eighteen eggs each; the resulting chicks are then combined for one hen to brood. Nests are similar to those provided for domestic chicks, except that finely pulverized earth is placed on the wooden floor and worked into a saucer-shaped disc which is then covered with an inch of straw or hay.

Lice are deadly enemies of young pheasants and so it's essential to be sure that the hen is free from all parasites, internal and external. She should be well dusted with pyrethrum powder or other louse powder before being placed on the nest. She should be dusted again in about a week and a third time around the seventeenth day of setting. No powder should be used within five days of the hatching date.

The hen should be allowed to leave the nest each morning to eat, drink, and dust. When she is ready, she will usually return voluntarily to resume her incubating vigil, though occasionally a hen must be caught up and returned to the nest.

Ordinarily, all eggs will hatch at about the same time. Eggshells should not be removed from the nest during the hatching period, since the empty shells seem to prevent the hen from resting too heavily upon the newly hatched chicks.

Since chicks do not immediately respond to the sounds made by the hen, as they would do in the case of a natural mother, their first reaction is to leave the nest. For this reason, they should be kept in the nest without food for twenty-four hours.

At the end of this time, hen and chicks can be removed to the brooder house and shut in for another twenty-four hours. Nests should be kept dark by means of sacking hung over openings during the hatching period, and the brooder house can be darkened in the same way for the first few hours of occupancy.

After one day in the nest and another in the brooder house, the chicks are given food in the form of starter mash, and are allowed access to a runway connected to the brooder house. The runway will serve as an exercise yard for a week or ten days, after which the young chicks can be transferred to the rearing pen.

Rearing pens for a backyard brood of chicks should be about sixteen feet square and five or six feet high, covered on the sides and top with one-inch hexagonal mesh poultry screen. They should be placed on green areas such as a field or lawn. Ground that has previously been used as range for domestic poultry should be avoided.

If setting hens are not available, day-old sexed chicks can be obtained and placed immediately in a brooder house with an electric brooder.

The following schedule is recommended for feeding chicks. On the second day in the brooder house, a small amount of starter mash is placed on a board. On the following day, starter mash on a tray may be placed near the hen so she will call the chicks and teach them to eat. If some of the chicks fail to eat by afternoon, the mash may be moistened with warm water or may be mixed with finely chopped hard-boiled eggs.

On the third day, a feedbox containing two-thirds mash and one-third fine chick scratch is introduced, though some feed is still placed on the original board. From the fourth to the fourteenth day the tray is eliminated and the chicks are fed the mash and scratch mixture in the feedbox, which is removed out of reach of the hen. Wheat and grit should be kept continuously in the pen to feed the hen, and of course a drinking fountain is located in the pen or runway.

During the third and fourth weeks the chicks' formula is changed to one-third starting mash, one-third growing pellets, and one-third scratch.

For the next five weeks, pellets and scratch are fed in proportion to the requirements of the growing chicks. Small grains and grit are also scattered in the vicinity of the pen.

It is also necessary to follow certain basic steps in the matter of sanitation. Hen droppings should be removed from the coop daily. Water should be changed frequently to insure a continuous supply and to prevent contamination. All sour or moldy feed should be removed, together with any dead birds. Maggots contain poisons deadly to chicks, and one dead bird can result in heavy mortality to the rest of the flock.

By the end of six weeks, the young birds should be well feathered and roosting outside the coop. The hen may be removed now, but the coop should be left in the rearing pen as a shelter for food and water. In extremely warm weather, a roof screen of brush or boughs placed in pen corners helps to maintain the birds' comfort.

A common problem in raising pheasants is overcrowding. After six weeks, penned pheasants require thirty square feet of space per bird. Tail picking and cannibalism can result from overcrowding. Blinders, clipping the tip of the upper bill, and adding green vegetables to the birds' diet help to check, but not cure, these harmful practices.

STOCKING

Several methods are used successfully in stocking pheasants. A number of private landowners and some gunning clubs prefer to liberate adult birds in the spring and let them breed and raise their families in natural surroundings.

Pheasants are by nature roamers, and so the first factor to be considered is that of adequate food and cover. There is little point in releasing birds into an area that is deficient in either of these necessities; without them the birds will leave. Such cover and food abundance in turn require ample space. At least three hundred acres should be available, and six hundred or more is better.

The optimum time to release spring birds is two or three weeks before the nesting season. This usually corresponds with the time of year when the first green vegetation is beginning to appear.

Birds should be transported to the liberation sites in crates, one cock and four or five hens to each pen. The crates should be placed close to cover and facing it. Before being released, the birds should be given time to quiet down, and it's a good idea to be able to open the pen by remote control, if possible, so that you can stand or hide some distance away.

Morning is the best time to liberate birds, giving them an entire day in which to acclimate themselves to their new surroundings. And choose fair weather for releases. Also, in releasing spring birds, it's wise to place a small amount of food near the cover for a few days to hold the birds close.

In a short time, the cocks will establish crowing territories and begin crowing to attract a harem of hens. In due course, nesting will occur and broods of chicks will hatch. Even under the most ideal conditions, a number of the resultant chicks and adults will die from accidents, disease, and predation, but from twenty to twenty-four hens and an equal number of cocks per each dozen hens liberated should survive to provide gunning by autumn. This method requires some predator control to insure a good survival rate.

A second stocking method is that of releasing three-month-old poults over a period from mid-August until mid-September. Feed is at its peak of abundance at this time of year, but even so, it is wise to augment the birds' natural diet with food placed near good cover to hold the birds in the area.

The poults should be strong on the wing by gunning season and will be sufficiently accustomed to their new life to provide sporty shooting. The only disadvantage to this method is the fact that pen-reared birds are more vulnerable to disease and to predators, which tend to stalk them at their feeding places. So, again, predator control is a must.

The third method of stocking adult birds to the gun is the one most often employed by state fish and game departments and shooting preserve owners. It is, of course, the most artificial method but, as mentioned earlier, birds released only days or even hours before they are hunted will exhibit many of the traits of wild birds as far as hiding and running are concerned.

However, these birds too are vulnerable to predators, and the longer they survive hunting pressure, the more they succumb to predation, at least during their first month or so of freedom. This is why pheasant shooting preserves stock birds for their customers on the morning of the hunt, scattering singles here and there over a wide area rather than in groups. And this is why state fish and game departments stock pheasants from time to time during the season rather than releasing their entire supply before the opening day. This method gives by far the best return on money spent.

A number of states have adopted still another stocking method in recent years. This is the trapping and transfer of wild pheasants into specific areas. It has been found that the trapping of various species of wildlife where they are plentiful (and sometimes unhuntable) and introducing them into areas devoid of the species, but where suitable habitat exists, is a useful management procedure. The classic example of such a project is demonstrated by Pennsylvania's wild-turkey restoration program, which has been copied by several other states.

In most states that carry on pheasant-rearing programs, the bulk of the birds are released on privately owned lands open to public shooting. But as natural habitat shrinks, especially in the East, increasing numbers of birds are being stocked on state-owned or leased lands acquired for the purpose of providing public shooting.

Releasing game farm birds into natural cover. They'll flush and run like their wild cousins, and those that survive the gunning season will quickly learn from their experiences. **Courtesy, Frank Woolner**

Massachusetts, for example, has a number of public shooting areas located strategically across the state. Necessarily, the quality of pheasant habitat varies among the different sites. But this factor is not as important here as it is in releasing birds on so-called "wild" lands, since these public shooting grounds' pheasants are stocked for one purpose only—to be harvested as quickly and as completely as possible.

Cocks are released in each cover at dusk. One weekly planting takes place Friday afternoons, and by dusk of Saturday evening the majority of birds stocked the day before repose in hunters' game bags. Bad weather in the form of sleet, snow, heavy rain, or wind can, of course upset the ratio of hunters' success, so there are more survivors some weekends than others. (There is no Sunday hunting in Massachusetts.) It is definitely put-and-take hunting, but at least it provides gunners a place to hunt and some birds to shoot at.

Even on the best weeks, there are always survivors. And it is these survivors, scattering and winging off into the woods and swamps on the perimeters of the shooting grounds, that provide some truly sporty shooting during ensuing days. It doesn't take a cock pheasant long to smarten up, once he has run the gantlet of Saturday gunners on a public shooting area.

One season a friend, Tom Thorne, invited me to shoot with him at Knightville, a state shooting area near my home. We went on a Tuesday morning and found only three or four cars in the parking area, although my companion declared that by eight o'clock on Saturday mornings it is almost impossible to find a place to park.

The release area is a river bottomland that stretches away behind a large flood-control dam. On both sides of the river, rank grasses grow chest high, and there are also some brambly fields bordering the bottomlands—ideal cover for pheasants to hide in. This is the area I would have hunted, but Tom shook his head.

"Last Saturday that swale looked and sounded like the second day of the battle of Gettysburg," he said. "There might be a cripple or two hiding in the grass down there, but all the healthy birds got the hell out of there by Saturday noon. And I think I know where to find one or two of them."

Instead of going down into the bottomland, he began following along the side of the hill overlooking it. Our way led through pine woods and rocky ledges alternating with laurel tangles and juniper, better-looking cover for rabbits than for pheasants. Below us I could see two men and a setter combing the high brown grass along the river.

We'd walked about a quarter of a mile when Tom's liver-and-white springer, Jill, struck scent. Her stub tail wiggled tentatively and then became a blur as she explored a patch of laurel. Belly to the ground, she crept into a sort of tunnel in the undergrowth, and suddenly, from the other end, a cock pheasant clattered into the air. As he slanted toward the valley below, Tom cut him down and Jill made an enthusiastic retrieve.

Only a hundred yards farther on, a frightened cock ran out of a clump of pines and flushed ahead of me. Jill collected this one too, when I dumped it with a straightaway shot. By noon Tom and I had our limit of two cocks apiece, taken from the brushy hillside, and we had bagged three woodcock as well.

HUNTING ON PRESERVES

Besides state-managed public hunting areas, there are today an increasing number of privately owned shooting preserves which provide pheasant hunting for a fee. These currently run from five to eight dollars per bird. Regulations vary among preserves as to the minimum number of birds a customer is obliged to buy.

Most preserves provide guides and dogs, some stipulating that if you use one of the preserve dogs, you only have to pay for the number of birds the dog finds. If you use your own dog, you must pay for the full number of birds contracted for, whether you find that number or not.

Preserves vary as widely as their rules, depending upon their size, quality of the cover, facilities, and, of course, the temperaments of their owners. On some the atmosphere and the shooting are highly artificial; others provide good hunting under almost natural conditions.

One thing all preserves share in common is providing places where hunters can enjoy their sport and be sure of finding birds to shoot at. Seasons are long—usually from September through March—and the number of birds shot, or at least shot at, is limited only by the amount of money the gunner wishes to pay. On most preserves, birds shot at but missed must be paid for.

There are some preserves, fortunately a minority, where pheasant shooting is akin to fishing for trout in a hatchery pool. Some provide what, to be charitable, can only be called marginal pheasant cover, and birds released on such property must be restrained to hold them until the gunner comes along.

I have seen preserves where pheasants were held in traps which could be sprung by the "guide" when the hunter came within range. And I have seen one where pheasants were placed under upside-down wire baskets. At the proper moment, the basket was kicked over and the pheasant took off, usually by air, but sometimes frustratingly on foot. I have been to more preserves, however, which offered good hunting under much more natural conditions.

A pheasant-shooting preserve should embrace a fairly large amount of territory, at least five hundred acres, and preferably more. Otherwise, a number of released birds will fly or run beyond its boundaries. Some are bound to do so anyway, of course, but the larger the preserve, the fewer birds it will lose in this manner.

Also, the larger the preserve, the more gunners it can support in safety. On a number of preserves, hunting groups are made up of a maximum of three gunners, who are allotted an area of a hundred acres or more at a safe distance from any other parties hunting the preserve at the same time.

A good preserve should provide a variety of choice pheasant cover consisting of grown-up and planted fields, hillsides, ravines, swamps, woodlots, or orchards, well-laced with brushy fencerows. If such cover does not exist naturally, it can be created by judicious planting of crops, grasses, fruits, and trees and letting nature take over in other areas.

The preserve owner should supply plump, healthy cocks and hens raised in pens that give them room to do some flying, thus making them strong on the wing.

On well-run preserves, birds ordered by the shooting parties are stocked in the covers shortly after daylight. They are not rocked and planted, but rather are released and allowed to fly freely wheresoever they will. Thus handled, they will run at the approach of danger, leaving scent for the dogs to follow, and they will flush with all the abandon of wild birds.

Besides conventional pheasant hunting, some preserves offer group fly-offs which provide fast and sporty shooting for those who want to try something a little different. Typical are the fly-offs conducted by Dutch Acres Preserve in North Chatham, New York. Groups of hunters numbering from a half dozen to fifteen or so participate in these shoots. The number of birds involved runs from a minimum of fifty up to a hundred or more.

Three-sided blinds are located in a circle around the release site, with one hunter assigned to each blind. The birds are brought to the release site in crates and are flown one at a time. By the time they reach the blinds they are moving at full throttle, especially with a tailwind behind them, and provide some very tricky shooting. It is much like pass shooting at doves or ducks. A party of better-than-average gunners can expect to score about 50 percent success on a fly-off.

Fly-offs generally take place in the morning and then, following lunch, the participants go out in groups with dogs to hunt the birds missed during the morning. By evening 90 to 95 percent of all birds released are usually harvested.

Preserve pheasant shooting may not be quite the same as hunting wild or semiwild birds in native covers, but it is certainly a lot better than no pheasant hunting at all, and on well-run preserves it affords gunners plenty of excitement and pleasure as well as far-better-than-average action. Preserves are excellent places to run hunting dogs for training and practice. And not the least of their attractions is the fact that, if you wish, they will swap you a dressed, frozen bird for each bird you shoot, thus doing away with the job of plucking and dressing your bag.

WILD PHEASANTS

There is no doubt that where conditions are conducive to the natural reproduction of pheasants, the resulting birds are far better specimens than their game-farm-reared counterparts. They are hardier, warier, more resistant to disease and predation, more fertile, and better able to cope with their environment. Even in states that must depend upon pen-reared birds to supply the demand, a substantial number of naturally propagated pheasants help to swell the annual crop.

Unfortunately, however, not all pheasant-hunting states have sufficient good habitat to produce an adequate supply of wild birds to take care of present-day gunning pressure. Those that do are fortunate, and their wildlife management personnel know it.

One of these favored states is South Dakota. Although pheasant populations have declined there, the state has never operated a game farm and has no intention of establishing one in the foreseeable future. Management personnel there have for some time had a trapping and transplant program in effect that places wild stock in suitable habitat throughout the state. They have also found that, as conditions improve in a given area, a core of resident birds will immediately bring about an increase in the population.

They have found, too, that game farm pheasants are expensive, owing to mortality all along the line. First there is the high death rate of chicks, then the mortality of the semidomesticated young birds, inexperienced in fending for themselves and easy prey for predators. South Dakota prefers to work on habitat improvement and, as long as the state remains agricultural to the extent that it is today, it will probably remain high on the list of top pheasant-producing states.

Nebraska is another state that can depend largely upon natural reproduction of pheasants. Wild populations of these birds are firmly established in the state. After their introduction some sixty years ago, their numbers climbed from a few thousand to four million in two decades. Under these favorable conditions, Nebraska wildlife management people feel that maintenance stocking, or stocking where a flourishing population already exists, is impractical for several reasons.

Natural laws control pheasant populations, among these the fact that a given area can support just so many birds. The land's carrying capacity is determined by environmental conditions and varies from year to year. Pheasants each spring produce more young than the land can support, nature's way of insuring the survival of the species. These surplus birds are doomed, and the addition of game farm birds only adds to this surplus.

Nebraska has also found wholesale stocking a high-cost business with a low return. The game commission stocked some 170,000 birds over a twelve-year period with a return of only 2½ percent to hunters at a cost of $16 a bird.

And, during the time that pheasants have been in Nebraska, natural selection has produced a hardy, resistant, and wary bird, well equipped to withstand the state's rigorous climate. Biologists believe that the risk of introducing disease or inferior genetic strains into these wild birds by stocking is reason enough to eschew such a program.

As a state spokesman declares, "Farmlands have and will continue to produce pheasants for a long time to come without a brooder house in the background. Habitat management," he adds, "is the key to abundance of any wildlife species, including pheasants, and only through a sound program can wildlife populations thrive."

This is in general the policy of the midwestern and western states and, given their favorable conditions, it is a fully justified one. Meanwhile, less fortunate states must continue to rely in part, at least, upon the game farm as a source of pheasants, though even in these states, habitat improvement can play a large role in increasing the supply.

At least we can be glad that these great game birds can be raised and released to provide hunting for millions of sportsmen across wide areas of the country where they cannot flourish naturally.

The Future

It is difficult to predict the future for anything today, including pheasant hunting. Changes in laws and attitudes—not to mention technology and environment—appear so fast in these times that it is hard to keep up with what *is* happening, to say nothing of trying to imagine what will happen tomorrow.

It was not always so. In the slower-paced and less technologically oriented eras in which our fathers and grandfathers lived, changes came more gradually, and it was possible to forecast with some chance of accuracy what might or might not happen. In those days it was possible to live a lifetime without drastic modifications in one's life-style or surroundings. Now it is only possible to suggest what could happen to any aspect of life as balanced against what may happen.

To look at the future of pheasant hunting necessitates considering the past history of all hunting in America. The story of the abundance of

130

wildlife the colonists found when they arrived in North America has been told too often to need repeating here. The exploitation and waste of our national resources by expanding populations moving westward is sadly familiar to all. The wholesale destruction of our native wildlife culminated in the bloody market hunting of the latter years of the past century, which saw the extinction of the passenger pigeon and the virtual obliteration of all but a remnant of the vast herds of bison and tremendous flocks of wildfowl that had inhabited this continent since prehistoric times.

Then, in the early years of the twentieth century, a new idea was born—conservation. Sparked by such pioneers as Theodore Roosevelt, Gifford Pinchot, John Muir, and other farseeing men, the emphasis changed from exploitation of natural resources to husbanding what was left and restoring what could be restored.

With this new spirit abroad in the land it seemed to interested men and women that a promising new era was at hand. Forward-looking steps were taken. Market hunting was banned, national parks, forests, and wildlife refuges were created across the country, and treaties were signed with other nations for the benefit of migrating species. The bright new era of conservation had arrived.

What its leaders and their army of followers did not foresee was the nullifying influence which the power and greed of special interests would exert upon their plans. From the beginning, the history of the conservation movement has been one of constant, often losing struggles against entrenched forces, outside and inside of government, which bitterly opposed any measures that adversely affected their own self-serving interests.

Timber men fought against lumbering restrictions designed to protect our national forests. Mining interests have battled for the right to strip government lands of mineral wealth. Ranchers and sheepmen have contended for what they believe to be their rightful prerogatives of destroying wildlife habitat by grazing and of exterminating wildlife on these lands by poisoning. With the help of unprincipled politicians, they have often succeeded in legislating their selfish, destructive programs into law. And over them all loom the monolithic bureaucracies of the Army Corps of Engineers and the Bureau of Reclamation, two agencies that have done far more damage to the face of our country than any outside enemy could have done. Between the two of them they have destroyed more wildlife and wildlife habitat in the process than the conservationists can restore in a thousand years.

Example: Less than one decade ago, the Corps of Engineers spent $30 million to straighten the meandering Kissimmee River, destroying forty thousand acres of wildlife-rich marshlands in the process, marshlands which strained out the natural and man-made solids which are now killing Lake Okeechobee, southern Florida's water supply. Now, water resource officials plan to spend $90 million more to restore the river to its former condition.

The corps will undoubtedly be given the job, thus receiving $120 million for destroying the Kissimmee River and then putting it back the way it was.

Example: The Bureau of Reclamation dreamed up a reservoir atop the Grand Canyon and went before Congress to ask for $1.5 billion to create a dam which would wipe out this natural wonder, along with a billion years of geologic history. So far they haven't received the money, but they don't give up easily.

It is true, of course, that if there had been no conservation movement, things would be far worse than they are today. No one can detract from the splendid accomplishments of generations of dedicated men and women in achieving worthwhile goals in conservation. But it is also true that the gains have been disappointing compared to what might have been accomplished with universal cooperation—rather than resistance from high places.

Nor does this opposition weaken. We have all seen it happen in our own lifetimes—the railroading of the Alaska pipeline, the pressure for offshore oil drilling, the recovery of shale oil, the green light for strip mining, the relaxation of air and water pollution regulations, the draining of irreplaceable wetlands, the widespread destruction caused by an expanding highway program, by "flood control" dams, power impoundments, nuclear reactors, irrigation projects which despoil rivers and flood vast areas of wildlife habitat, by dredging and channeling—all undertaken to profit insatiable corporate interests and pork-barreling politicians. Nor are these crimes against the environment likely to decrease with the passing years.

Shoulder to shoulder with these irresponsible destroyers stand the "developers" to whom any empty patch of land, however small, is an irresistible invitation to place upon it a housing development, a shopping center, a hotel, motel, rest home, amusement park, ski area, or high-rise condominium. And today these voracious profiteers are not content with a few acres here and there; today they must spread new communities, instant towns, and mini-cities across the land. Each year their frenzied activities destroy millions of acres of prime wildlife habitat.

So much for the problems of our waters and lands, upon which pheasants and all wildlife depend for their existence. There are other problems as well.

One problem is the growing antihunting sentiment which has become a real threat to the sport of hunting. Apparently, these ill-informed zealots believe that, were it not for hunters, wild creatures would lead an idyllic existence of frolicking together in flower-strewn fields and woodlands, surrounded by bountiful food, warmth, comfort, and love until at last they died of old age. In their bright world of pretense, no pheasant chicks would ever be swallowed by snakes, no bunny rabbits torn to pieces by foxes or owls, no squirrels crushed by speeding cars, no deer starve to death in winter snows.

True, the members of this cult enjoy steaks, prime ribs, roast lamb and pork, not to mention poultry, as well as anyone else does, but this, of course, is different. Somehow, in their specious reasoning, the conversion of these creatures from living organisms to chops and roasts is accomplished by some benign force that sets it apart from the conversion of deer into venison or rabbits into a game pie.

It would not do any good to attempt to enlighten these individuals concerning the fundamentals of wildlife management—that game is a crop like wheat or carrots, that a given area can support just so many pheasants, just as a given field can raise only so many potatoes, and that the surplus birds in that area are doomed to death from disease or starvation. It would do no good to attempt to impart such information because their beliefs are based on emotion rather than reason.

And unfortunately, through the media and organized promotion, the antigun faction has been able to make considerable impact upon the hunting scene. Using the "big lie" tactics so successful for other propagandists in recent times, they have managed to gain a considerable following. They have found a forum in the schools, the media, and even the courts. From a mere nuisance they have of late become a real threat to the future of all hunting.

Closely leagued with them, sometimes so closely that the dividing line is invisible are the antigun groups whose goal it is to make it illegal for American citizens to use or even to own firearms. This group contains a surprising number of lawmen as well as legislators among its supporters.

Despite the complete lack of logic in their pronouncements, the antigun forces are gaining converts to their ranks, and their activities, too, constitute a threat to the future of hunting. Their danger is real and continuing, and hunters had better face up to them.

This is the context in which the future of pheasant hunting must be considered. This is the first line of conservation for pheasant hunters. But the chances of preserving and improving our sport aren't as slim as they might seem, if we are willing to act.

In the matter of keeping our guns, the solution lies largely in the fields of public education and public relations. There is no way of knowing how many antigun people there are in the country, but we do know that there are some 25 million licensed hunters. They probably outnumber the gun controllers by a ratio of at least four or five to one.

Twenty-five million hunters translates into 25 million voters plus their families, and comprises a sizable bloc whose sentiments would be respected by legislators at both federal and state levels—providing they made these sentiments known. This is where the hunting fraternity has frequently not shown to best advantage. We have been too silent a majority. We have preferred to leave the fight to someone else and to remain deaf to the strident and vociferous voices of a minority.

The time has come when we must all lift up our voices to drown out the opposition. One of the most powerful voices raised in our behalf is that of the National Rifle Association. Besides its efficient lobbying in federal and state capitals, the NRA disseminates straight-from-the-shoulder facts to counteract the distorted propaganda of the gun controllers. Every man who carries a hunting license should also carry a membership in this association.

Other worthwhile and respected organizations include the National Wildlife Federation, the Wildlife Society, the Boone and Crockett Club, and the Izaak Walton League, among others.

Besides supporting conservation-oriented organizations, there are other things we can do. We must attend gun legislation hearings and make our feelings known, or at least take the time to contact our representatives and senators to let them know our sentiments when antigun bills are introduced.

Sportsmen's clubs can be potent forces, too, if they would only put away the poker chips and stop bickering over whether rabbits are more important than hares, and whether they should stock brook, brown, or rainbow trout.

A gun has been a precious possession of Americans since colonial times and remains so today. Judging from the number of youngsters who enroll in hunter safety courses as a step toward obtaining a hunting license, guns and gunning are still very much a part of the American scene, and it is up to us to keep them so in order that these youngsters may claim their rightful heritage.

Education and public relations are also the most effective weapons in combating the misinformation broadcast by the Friends of Animals and their ilk, organized and unorganized. Courses related to wildlife, ecology, and other environmental sciences would go far to counteract the "Bambi syndrome" among young people. Youngsters who grow up knowing the true story of the birth, life, and death of wild creatures, their habits and their struggles, are not likely to be deceived by the lies of the anti-hunting people, or to enroll themselves among the ranks of these nature fakirs when they become adults.

In former times, boys and girls raised on farms and in small communities grew up close to wild creatures. Today, however, many children grow up without ever seeing a raccoon or a fox outside a zoo.

The antihunting people take full-page ads in newspapers and appear on TV to rant against hunters and hunting. Why can't the gunning fraternity use these same media to tell the truth about hunting? Congress has in recent years set aside a National Hunting and Fishing Day dedicated to hunters and fishermen, featuring displays and programs put on by sportsmen's organizations. We need to get our side across to the public and not allow the opposition to do all the talking.

The nonhunting public should be informed that it is hunters who have

The future of pheasant hunting is in the hands of hunters. Photo by author

insisted on the protection of wildlife species over the years, and it is hunters who pay for this protection as well as for law enforcement, habitat improvement, wildlife research, and management programs, all from taxes on guns and ammunition, from license fees and outright gifts to wildlife-oriented organizations. What have the do-gooders contributed except misinformation?

All of which brings us to the subject of finding a place to hunt pheasants. One place where a lot of people are going to find their hunting in the future, especially in heavily populated areas, is on privately owned shooting preserves, and it is fortunate that pheasants lend themselves so well to this kind of hunting.

Besides these preserves, state-owned public shooting areas are going to provide more opportunities for hunting in the years to come, and it is encouraging to note how many states have recognized this trend and are acquiring as much land as possible in the face of skyrocketing real estate prices. Encouraging, too, is the amount of acreage being given or left to the states for this purpose by interested citizens. Here again, pheasants by nature are one of the easiest and most successful of all species to stock on these lands.

However, despite the expansion of shooting preserves and state-managed shooting areas, privately owned farmlands must still play their role in providing hunting opportunities, as they do today. This involves the thorny subject of posted lands, which will be a continuing problem in the future. Since pheasants are birds of the farmlands, pheasant hunters in pursuit of their sport come into closer contact with farmers than is the case with grouse and woodcock gunners, and sometimes the results of these contacts have been unfortunate.

Among the followers of any sport there are invariably a minority of selfish clods, devoid of any sense of sportsmanship, whose only concern is their own enjoyment. And the ranks of hunters have their full complement of these undesirables. These are the goons who trample mowings, cut barbed-wire fences, shoot pheasants in dooryards, and, if no pheasants are available, sometimes even turn their guns on family pets and livestock.

A lot of prime pheasant habitat is posted against trespassing as a result. Often, the hunter who asks owners of posted lands for permission to hunt will have his request granted, especially if he goes before the season to make his arrangements. Gun goons almost never ask permission to hunt.

A number of states have formed cooperative agreements among landowners whereby permit hunting is allowed. The state issues the permits and sees to it that regulations are adhered to. Still other landowners are permitting hunting for a fee, which will probably become an even more prevalent practice in the future. And more and more sportsmen's clubs today are banding together to lease or buy land which is then posted against nonmembers. It may not be democratic, but it is a trend, and for those who can afford it, this may become a solution to the problem of finding hunting room in the future.

One thing is certain. It is going to be harder to find places to hunt in the years ahead than it has been in the past. Farmlands will be scarcer. But they can be made to yield larger crops of birds, just as a scientifically cultivated field can be made to yield additional wheat or potatoes. The science of wildlife management, like the science of agriculture, has advanced markedly in recent years and will doubtless continue to do so.

Biologists have learned how to manage wildlife resources to achieve the greatest possible yield. One of their most effective tools is habitat improvement. The game farm will have to continue to play its part in many states, but habitat improvement will remain the most important factor in the propagation of pheasants in the future.

Fortunately, today an increasing number of farmers are coming to realize that wildlife management includes the conservation of soil and water as well as the production of game. They have come to appreciate, too, the real value of small game on their lands and are willingly cooperating with the biologists to keep the wildlife there.

Habitat improvement, as it applies to pheasants, consists of several factors, all related to the basic requirements of food, water, and cover.

Creating small areas of cover has been found to be a simple and effective method of improving pheasant habitat. These patches may be only a rod square, but several of them strategically placed in different sections of a farm are more valuable than one or two large areas. They can be located so that they will benefit the birds and yet not affect tillable acreage—corners of fields, rocky ground, and steep slopes, for example. Establishing small feeding covers allows the birds access to food and also plays a part in the control of erosion.

Besides feed patches, it is well to create small brushy areas such as patches of high weeds, spring runs, and short lengths of streams in pasturelands. Shrubs and cut brush may be used to supplement cover already in existence. Large brush piles scattered here and there are helpful. So are brushy corridors to provide travel lanes.

Nesting cover is important, too, and can be provided by furnishing small areas of grasslands, protecting them from fire and from the use of herbicides and pesticides. Leaving brushy fencerows bordering fields and along roadsides is a practice that will also increase and hold pheasant populations. Farmers should be encouraged to delay mowing hay and weed fields until after hens are off the nests in early July.

The drying up of springs and streams in midsummer droughts can drive pheasants from the best of habitat, and for this reason it is good practice to dig out spring seeps and construct pools in streams which will provide necessary water for resident birds. If these various areas are fenced, it will provide some protection from predators for birds using them. All these measures will help stocked birds to survive and wild pheasants to reproduce and thrive.

There are still many factors of pheasant management that remain to be researched and developed, but the wildlife biologists are working on these problems, and there is no reason to believe that further advances will not keep pace with our need.

Pheasants have shown themselves to be hardy, adaptable birds. They have survived civilization for several thousand years and, given the advantages of wise management, they will doubtless continue to be part of the American scene for a long time to come.

INDEX

Pages in *italics* indicate illustrations.

DATE DUE